THE NEXUS OF GOVERNMENTAL INTEGRITY AND THE SURVIVABILITY OF AMERICAN CONSTITUTIONAL DEMOCRACY

THE NEXUS OF GOVERNMENTAL INTEGRITY AND THE SURVIVABILITY OF AMERICAN CONSTITUTIONAL DEMOCRACY

RELIGION AND LAW SERIES, VOLUME FOUR

George J. Gatgounis

WIPF & STOCK · Eugene, Oregon

THE NEXUS OF GOVERNMENTAL INTEGRITY AND THE SURVIVABILITY OF AMERICAN CONSTITUTIONAL DEMOCRACY

Religion and Law Series, Volume Four

Copyright © 2022 George J. Gatgounis. All rights reserved. Except for brief quotations in critical publications or reviews, no part of this book may be reproduced in any manner without prior written permission from the publisher. Write: Permissions, Wipf and Stock Publishers, 199 W. 8th Ave., Suite 3, Eugene, OR 97401.

Wipf & Stock
An Imprint of Wipf and Stock Publishers
199 W. 8th Ave., Suite 3
Eugene, OR 97401

www.wipfandstock.com

PAPERBACK ISBN: 978-1-7252-6125-9
HARDCOVER ISBN: 978-1-7252-6126-6
EBOOK ISBN: 978-1-7252-6127-3

VERSION NUMBER 011022

CONTENTS

INTRODUCTION | xi

GOVERNMENTAL SURVIVABILITY DERIVES FROM ITS INTEGRITY, CREDIBILITY, LEGITIMACY, TRANQUILITY, AND ECONOMIC EFFICIENCY | 1
    Introduction | 1
        The Interrelation of Law and Morality | 1
        A Government, as a Community of Principle, Must Be Moral to Survive | 2
    Integrity a Gateway to Credibility | 3
        Integrity of the American Political System | 3
        Integrity of the Persons in the American Political System | 8
            Personal Integrity: The Conscience Model | 8
            Personal Fiduciaries: The Trust Model | 9
            The Present Need for Integrity-Fostering Devices | 12
    Credibility A Gateway to Legitimacy | 14
        Credibility Defined as a Positive Social Consensus | 14
        Legitimization through Credibility Defined | 16
        Credibility Described as an Abstraction or Myth | 17
            Social Illustrations of Legitimization | 19
            Management Illustrations of Legitimization | 20
            Military Illustrations of Legitimization | 23
    Domestic Tranquility a Gateway to Economic Efficiency | 24
    Conclusion: The Essential Links in the Political Chain Holding Together a Constitutional Republic | 25

    The Essential Links in the Chain: Integrity, Credibility, Legitimacy, Tranquility, and Efficiency | 25
    Representative Democracy, Verity, and Survivability | 26

MAJOR CASE IN POINT: THE FRAGMENTATION OF GORBACHEV'S GOVERNMENT | 27
  Introduction | 27
  Statement of Thesis | 28
  Gorbachev's Presidency Governed A System Already Fragmenting: How It Teetered on Collapse | 28
    The Vulnerability of the Monolith | 29
      Vulnerability Because of Its Structural Flaw: Absence of Checks and Balances | 29
      Vulnerability Because of a Minimized External Threat | 31
      Vulnerability Because of Its Economic Plight | 32
    The Complex of Diverging Forces in Motion | 33
      Economic Stagnation | 33
      Reactionary Conservatism | 35
      Resurgent Nationalism | 37
      Political Liberalism | 39
      An Awakened Sense of History and Its Lessons | 42
  Once *Perestroika* and *Glasnost* Were in Motion, Gorbachev's Presidency No Longer Led but Was Led | 43
    What Gorbachev Tried to Do | 43
      Rule from a Deteriorating Center | 43
    Insight from the Reaction to Gorbachev: What the Putsch Tried to Undo | 45
  An Analysis of the Hapless Initiator of the Revolution: Who Was Gorbachev Politically? | 46
    Was He a Communist? | 46
    Was He Religious? | 48
    Was He a Democrat? | 50
    Was He Incompetent? | 51
  Concluding Remarks: Comparing What Gorbachev Tried tto Do and What Happened | 53
    What Was Gorbachev's Vision for the New Nation? | 53

The Presidency's Epitaph: Deux Ex Machina | 54

FOCUS ON MCNAMARA AND VIETNAM: INTEGRITY, CREDIBILITY, AND LEGITIMACY IN DOWNWARD DEMISE | 56
   The Moral Question on Mcnamara: Was He Morally Culpable? | 57
   The Personal Question on Mcnamara: What Made Him Tick? | 61
     McNamara's Mind | 61
     McNamara's Heart | 62
   Excursus: Omissions in Both Works | 63
   Conclusion: The Irony of the Mcnamara Legacy | 64
     Compromise of Presidential Integrity—Presidential Buck Shifting: Exculpatory Panacea or Admission of Breached Duty? | 66

THE LINE DIVIDING GOVERNMENTAL POWERS: A LINE OF SEPARATION OR HERMETIC ISOLATION? | 69
   Referents by Which the Line Divides | 69
     Inherent Authority | 69
     Specific Actions | 70
   Examples of the Line's Severance | 70
   Examples Where the Line Is Not Yet Clearly Drawn | 71
     An Example of Civil Disobedience against a Governmental Body with Dubious Credibility | 72
     An Example of Civil Non-Compliance with a Governmental Agency with Dubious Sensitivity: Making OSHA Work by Disengaging the Adversarial Relationship | 75

HOW CIVIL RELIGION AND GOVERNMENTAL INTEGRITY INTERPLAY: AN ANALYSIS OF MICHAEL J. PERRY'S LOVE & POWER: THE ROLE OF RELIGION AND MORALITY IN AMERICAN POLITICS | 79
   Introduction and Statement of Thesis | 79
   Analysis | 80
     Premises | 80
     Scope | 81

Ideal | 83
Means | 84
Critique | 85
Conclusion | 87
The Relation of Governmental Integrity and Religion | 88
   Introduction: The Need for Resolution of Past Ambiguity | 88
      The Task of Definition Is Imperative | 88
      The Task of Definition Is Problematic | 90
   Scope and Statement of Thesis | 93
      Delimitations | 93
      Statement of Thesis | 95
   Retrospect: A Précis of the Supreme Court's Act of Defining Constitutionally Protected Religion | 96
   The Pre-Seeger Theistic Phase (1789–1964) | 96
   First Key Development in 1789: The First Amendment's Adoption | 96
      Illumination from the Alternate Drafts of the First Amendment's Religion Clauses | 96
      The Apparent Exclusion of Non-Theistic Faiths | 99
   The Second Key Development in 1878–90: The Mormon Polygamy Cases | 100
      Reynolds v. United States (1878) | 100
      Beason v. United States (1890) | 101
      The Late Corporation of the Church of Jesus Christ of Latter-day Saints v. United States (1890) | 102
   The Post-Seeger Non-Theistic Phase (Post-1965) | 103
   Key Developments in 1940, 1948, and 1952 Leading to Seeger: The Conscientious Objector Cases | 103
      Conflict in the Lower and Supreme Courts before 1965 | 103
         Kauten v. United States in the Second Circuit (1940) | 103
         United States v. Ballard in the Supreme Court (1944) | 104
         George v. United States in the Ninth Circuit (1952) | 105
      Resolution by the Supreme Court in *Seeger* in 1965 | 107
         The United States v. Seeger Highmark (1965) | 108
         Welsh v. United States (1970) | 110

More Recent Key Developments | 111
  United States v. Yoder: The Amish School Exemption Case
    (1972) | 111
  Malnak v. Maharishi Yogi: The Third Circuit Amalgam of the
    Yoder and Seeger Definitions (1979) | 112
  Africa v. American Christian Movement for Life (MOVE): The
    Third Circuit's Four-Point Definition (1981) | 113
A Summary of Definitional Development: Current Qualifiers of
  Constitutionally Protected Religion | 115
  Negative Qualifiers | 115
  Positive Qualifiers | 116
Prospect—Toward Parameters for Future Clarity: The Need for
  Clarity in Forthcoming Definitions | 117
  The Challenge of Clarity | 117
  The Challenge Philosophically | 118
  The Challenge Constitutionally | 118
Suggested Parameters for a Future Clarity | 119
  Specificity | 121
    Specificity Because of the Plethora of Vague Definitions | 121
    Specificity as a Device for Screening Cases | 122
  Flexibility | 123
    The Argument for a Flexible Scope | 124
      The Need for a Flexible Scope Because of the Inviolability of
        Conscience | 124
      The Need for a Flexible Scope Because of the Growth and Diver-
        sification of Religious Beliefs | 124
      The Need for a Flexible Scope Because of the Danger of the Chill-
        ing Effect | 124
  Uniformity | 125
    The Argument for a Bifurcated Definition | 125
    The Argument for Uniform Definition | 127
  An Analytical Framework Rather than a Conventional
    Definition | 127
  Concluding Remarks: A Plea to the Legal Community | 128

CONCLUSION | 130

INTRODUCTION

The American government is in a state of crisis—a crisis of integrity. But how important is an integrity crisis? Is it more important than an international crisis, a natural disaster, a pandemic, an economic crash?

Governments that are not trusted do not survive. A government must have credibility to survive. Even if the government stays in power by aiming guns to the heads of the people, that government will not survive as soon the guns are no longer loaded.

Governments must have integrity, because without integrity, they will lack credibility; without credibility, they will lack legitimacy. Illegitimate governments lack survivability.

In this day of crisis, the bottom line is the survivability of American constitutional democracy. This government must have integrity to maintain credibility. The American system of government remains, by and large, because the people whom it governs want it. This work outlines links on a chain—integrity, credibility, legitimacy, tranquility, and survivability. America needs all the links of this chain to hang on into the next millennium.

GOVERNMENTAL SURVIVABILITY DERIVES FROM ITS INTEGRITY, CREDIBILITY, LEGITIMACY, TRANQUILITY, AND ECONOMIC EFFICIENCY

INTRODUCTION

The Interrelation of Law and Morality

"In civilized life, law floats in a sea of ethics."[1] Byron White concurs that "the law is constantly based on notions of morality."[2] Theoretical morality leads to law. Cicero sees law as the morality embedded in human nature springing into sociopolitical norms: "Whoever is disobedient is fleeing from himself and denying his human nature, and by reason of this very fact he will suffer the worst penalties, even if he escapes what is commonly considered punishment."[3] Although the term "law" connotes rules, constraints, norms enforced by states, sanctions for violations, permanency, and legitimacy,[4] the term "law" also connotes morality, because

1. Earl Warren, *The New York Times*, Nov. 23, 1962.
2. Byron R. White, majority opinion, Bowers v. Hardwick, June 30, 1986.
3. Marcus Tullius Cicero, *De Re Publica* (1943), book 3, paragraph 22, 211.
4. Unpublished lecture notes, STM-805, "Law and Public Policy," Harvard Kennedy School of Government, Professor Cary Coglianese, September 26,

law derives from some moral philosophy. Another modern legal commentator posits that "judicial reasoning in concrete cases must proceed from society's set of moral principles and ideals."[5] As Dworkin argues: "moral principle is the foundation of law."[6]

Law derives from morality, but conversely, morality also derives from law. Although John F. Kennedy's televised statement on June 11, 1963, that "law alone cannot make men see right" rings true today, law that is moral, if observed, leads to morality.[7] "Because just as good morals, if they are to be maintained, have need of the laws, so the laws, if they are to be observed, have need of good morals," according to Machiavelli.[8] Both Cicero and Machiavelli see a self-sustaining cycle—social morality leads to legal morality; legal morality reinforces social morality. As Cicero explains:

> And there will not be different laws at Rome and at Athens, or different laws now and in the future, but one eternal and unchangeable law will be valid for all actions and all times, and there will be one master and rule, that is God, over us all, for he is the author of this law, its promulgator, and its enforcing judge."[9]

Law and morality necessarily interact and interreact.

A Government, as a Community of Principle, Must Be Moral to Survive

In a government, a concert of principle which centralizes integrity in politics is an effective gateway to legitimacy.[10] Without legiti-

---

1994.

5. Harry Wellington, "Common Law Rules and Constitutional Double Standards: Some Notes on Adjudication" (1973), 83 Yale L.J. 221, 244.

6. Ronald D. Dworkin, Law's Empire, 1986.

7. John F. Kennedy, televised speech on June 11, 1963.

8. Niccoló Machiavelli, *Discourses on the First Decade of Titus Livius*, trans. Allan Gilbert (1965), book I, chapter 18, 241.

9. Marcus Tullius Cicero, *De Re Publica* (1943), book 3, paragraph 22, 211.

10. Cf. Ronald Dworkin, *Law's Empire* (1986), 216.

GOVERNMENTAL SURVIVABILITY DERIVES FROM ITS INTEGRITY

mization, a government will not survive. Robert Alan Dahl, in his seminal *The Preface to Democratic Theory*, argues that law is not what holds nations together; rather, cultural values and prevailing social conditions sustain an undergirding belief in the legitimacy of law. A sense of legitimacy in a representative democracy derives from moral consensus. A belief in the legitimacy and moral correctness of law superintends obedience to it.[11] In the same vein, John Courtney Murray argues that moral and religious consensus must come before a legal order.[12] Purcell agrees with Dahl's point that it is much more plausible to suppose the American Constitution has survived because American society is essentially democratic, rather than suppose that American society remains democratic because of the Constitution.[13] Until the American government loses its credibility with the American people, the American government will survive. The integrity of both the American political system and its politicians is the essential key to its credibility with American society. The American government's integrity is its only gateway to social credibility, political legitimacy, domestic tranquility, and economic efficiency—and ultimately its own survivability.

INTEGRITY A GATEWAY TO CREDIBILITY

Integrity of the American Political System

A government, as a political system, must have integrity to be credible to the governed. More specifically, the political system must have the integrity to govern, not tyrannize. Tyranny occurs whenever human rights are violated—whenever the right to life, liberty, and property is impinged without "due process of law." Although

---

11. Lynn Sharp Paine, "Managing for Organizational Integrity," *Harvard Business Review*, March 1994.

12. C.E. Curran and R.A. McCormick, S.J. eds., *Readings in Moral Theology No. 7* (New York: Paulist Press). Part III, John Courtney Murray, S.J., "The Doctrine Lives: The Eternal Return of Natural Law," 184–220.

13. Edward A. Purcell, Jr., *The Crisis of Democratic Theory* (1973), 260–61.

the American founding fathers faced an "almost totally uncharted course,"[14] they crafted the quintessential political system—a constitutional federalism with tripartite separation of powers under the umbrella of a bill of substantive rights. The founding fathers built a system most likely to govern and least likely to tyrannize.

The Madisonian logic undergirding the American political system was impeccable—if unrestrained by external checks, any given individual or group of individuals will tyrannize others.[15] To Madison, an "external check" for an individual consists of the "application of rewards and penalties or the expectation that they will be applied, by some source other than the given individual himself."[16] Further, as an empirical generalization, Madison understood that the accumulation of all powers, legislative, executive, and judiciary, in the same hands implies the elimination of external checks. The elimination of external checks produces tyranny. Therefore the accumulation of all powers in the same hands implies tyranny.[17] Moreover, if unrestrained by external checks, a minority of individuals will tyrannize a majority of individuals.[18] Conversely, if unrestrained by external checks, a majority of individuals will tyrannize a minority of individuals.[19] As Hamilton expressed the principle succinctly, "Give all power to the many, they will oppress the few. Give all power to the few, they will oppress the

---

14. Paul Simon, *Advice and Consent* (1992), 152.

15. Robert A. Dahl, *A Preface to Democratic Theory* (1956), 6; Dahl's rendition of Madison's "Observations," of April 1787, in *The Complete Madison: His Basic Writings*, ed. Saul K. Padover (1953), pp. 27–29; letter to Jefferson, October 24, 1787, 40–43.

16. "Observations," of April 1787, in *The Complete Madison*, 7–29; letter to Jefferson, 40–43.

17. *The Federalist*, ed. Edward Mead Earle ("The Modern Library" New York: Random House, n.d.), 313.

18. Dahl's rendition of Madison as per *The Debates in the Several State Conventions on the Adoption of the Federal Constitution as Recommended by the General Convention at Philadelphia*, in 1787, together with *The Journal of Federal Convention*, etc., ed. Jonathan Elliot (2d ed.; Phil.: Lippincott, 1941), V, 203.

19. Ibid.

many."²⁰ Madison's understanding of a representative democracy, a republic, was a governmental system which derives all of its powers directly or indirectly from the great body of the people and is administered by persons holding their office during the pleasure of that body, for a limited period, or during good behavior.²¹

A variety of delegates to the Constitutional convention perceived basic human nature as a ravenous power monger. Lenoir, in the North Carolina debates, warned that "we ought to consider the depravity of human nature, the predominant thirst of power which is in the breast of everyone, the temptations rulers may have."²² Franklin, at the Federal Convention, joined the chorus: "There are two passions which have a powerful influence on the affairs of men. These are ambition and avarice; the love of power and the love of money."²³ Hamilton, at the Federal Convention, agreed that "men love power."²⁴ Mason articulated the same perspective at the Federal Convention: "From the nature of man, we may be sure that those who have power in their hands . . . will always, when they can . . . increase it."²⁵ Jefferson, said "one hundred and seventy-three despots would surely be as oppressive as one . . . an elective despotism was not the government we fought for."²⁶ Not forgetting ample historical examples of despotism, the founding fathers concluded human nature was inherently dangerous because of an inherent lust for power.

Accordingly, in Madisonian epistemology, at least two conditions are necessary for the existence of a non-tyrannical republic: First, the accumulation of all powers, legislative, executive, and judiciary, in the same hands—whether of one, a few, or many and

20. *The Debates in the Several State Conventions,* together with *The Journal of Federal Convention,* 203.
21. *The Federalist,* No. 39.
22. IV, 204.
23. V, 145.
24. V, 200.
25. V, 294.
26. *The Federalist,* No. 48, 324.

whether hereditary, self-appointed, or elected—must be avoided.[27] Second, factions must be so controlled that they do not succeed in acting adversely to the rights of other citizens or to the permanent and aggregate interests of the community.[28] A faction is a number of citizens, whether amounting to a majority or a minority of the whole, who are "united and actuated by some common impulse or passion, or of interest, adverse to the rights of other citizens, or to the permanent and aggregate interests of the community."[29] The problems of power accumulation by a faction are legion.

If factions are to be limited in power accumulation, constitutional controls must curb the effects of faction. If a faction consists of less than a majority, it can be controlled by the operation of the "republican principle" of voting in the legislative body—that is, the majority can vote down the minority. The development of a majority faction can be limited if the electorate is "numerous, extended, and diverse in interests."[30] Extend the sphere, and you take in a greater variety of parties and interests; you will make it less probable that a majority of the whole will have a common motive to invade the rights of other citizens; or if such common motive exists, it will be more difficult to act in unison, hence tyrannically.[31] As Dahl summarizes Madison:

> The probability that any given individual or group will tyrannize over others if unrestrained by external checks is sufficiently high so that if tyranny is to be avoided over a long period, the constitutionally prescribed machinery of any government must maintain some external checks on all those holding power.[32]

The distinction between internal and external checks is significant, because internal checks vary with the individual. Internal

---

27. *The Federalist*, No. 47, 313.
28. *The Federalist*, No. 10, 57ff.
29. *The Federalist*, No. 10, 54.
30. Dahl at 16; *The Federalist*, No. 10, 54.
31. *The Federalist*, No. 10, 61.
32. Dahl at 19.

checks—the conscience (superego), attitudes, and basic predispositions—are crucial in determining whether any given individual will tyrannize others. These internal checks vary from individual to individual, from social group to social group, and from time to time. Therefore, the probability of tyranny emerging in a society is the extent to which various types of internalized responses are present among members of that society.[33]

Separation of powers prevents tyranny because it provides an external check upon the tyrannical impulses of officials. Separation of powers provides an external check because it guarantees that the ambitions of individuals in one branch will counteract those in another. Countermanding ambitions will be effective because the individuals in one branch can invoke the threat of rewards and punishments against tyrannical individuals in the other branch or branches.[34]

Further, the Constitution prevents the legislature from tyrannizing the minority. As Hamilton posited:

> No legislative act, contrary to the Constitution, can be valid. To deny this would be to affirm that the deputy is greater than his principle; that the servant is above the master; that the representatives of the people are superior to the people themselves; that men acting by virtue of powers may do not only what their powers forbid.[35]

Hamilton, therefore, envisioned Constitutional law as a permanent check upon tyranny.

---

33. Dahl at 18; *The Federalist*, No. 10, 61.
34. Dahl at 20.
35. *Federalist Papers*, No. 78, 467.

THE NEXUS OF GOVERNMENTAL INTEGRITY AND THE SURVIVABILITY

Integrity of the Persons in the American Political System

Personal Integrity: The Conscience Model

"To no one will we sell, to no one will we refuse or delay the right to justice"—Magna Carta.[36] Integrity in government must issue from the persons who compose it. Governments will neither function nor survive without integrity on the personal level.[37] In the words of Melancton Smith, representatives of the people must have personal integrity.

> The idea that naturally suggests itself to our minds, when we speak of representatives, is that they resemble those they represent; they should be a true picture of the people; possess the knowledge of the circumstances and their wants; sympathize in all their distresses, and be disposed to seek their true interests.[38]

As Dworkin substantiates:

> Here, then, is our case for integrity, our reason for striving to see, so far as we can, both its legislative and adjudicative principles vivid in our political life. A community of principle accepts integrity. It condemns checkerboard statutes and less dramatic violations of that ideal as violating the associative character of its deep organization.... Internally compromised statutes... serve the incompatible aim of a rulebook community, which is to compromise convictions along lines of power.[39]

Accordingly, the representatives of the people must have integrity to earn and maintain credibility.

---

36. As quoted by Peter G. Brown, *Restoring the Public Trust* (1994), 69.

37. Consider Arthur I. Applbaum's stunning discussion, "Systems of Deception: The Ethics of Lying When Everyone Is Doing It," unpublished seminar notes in "The Ethics of Truthfulness in Management: Notes, Cases, and Readings."

38. John A. Rohr, *To Run a Constitution: The Legitimacy of the Administrative State* (1986), 46.

39. Ronald Dworkin, *Law's Empire* (1986), 214.

GOVERNMENTAL SURVIVABILITY DERIVES FROM ITS INTEGRITY

Thus, in Dworkin's reasoning, integrity is a distinct political ideal. Because the American people desire to be a community governed by a "single vision of justice and fairness and procedural due process," the American people accept the adjudicative principle of integrity as sovereign over law. The principle of integrity as sovereign over law "makes no sense except among people who want fairness and justice."[40] The American people, in Dworkin's view, desire an association of principle.[41] In a community of free and independent people, who disagree about political morality and wisdom, the principle of integrity offers an attractive basis for claims of political legitimacy, as well as a framework for unity.[42] If a community organizes itself around the principle of integrity, the community develops into one of principle. In Dworkin's theory, a "genuine associative community" of principle can claim moral legitimacy.[43]

Personal Fiduciaries: The Trust Model

The functionaries of the American political system must act as trustees to the American people because they have a fiduciary relation to them. Disraeli also sees the fiduciary dimension of political power.

> All power is a trust ... we are accountable for its exercises; that, from the people, and for the people all springs, and all must exist.[44]

Locke sees the people as judge of those who govern them.

---

40. Dworkin, 263.
41. Dworkin, 404.
42. Dworkin, 411.
43. Dworkin, 214.
44. Benjamin Disraeli, Vivian Grey, quoted by Peter G. Brown, *Restoring the Public Trust* (1994), preface.

> The people shall be judge: for who shall be judge whether the trustee ... acts well and according to the trust reposed in him, but he who deputes him.[45]

The trust relationship recognizes the direct duty of the government to preserve and enhance the well-being of all persons under its aegis. Locke sees the trust relationship as central to natural law—"the law of nature to be observed, which willeth the peace and preservation of all mankind."[46] The trust model holds that the legislator (and the executive) must discharge these obligations to the public good on the basis of impartial deliberation. As Locke elaborates:

> Whenever ... the legislative shall transgress this fundamental rule of society, and either by ambition, fear, folly, or corruption, endeavor to grasp themselves or put into the hands of any other absolute power over the lives, liberties, and estates of the people, by this breach of trust they forfeit the power the people had put into their hands.[47]

The fiduciary conception imposes an obligation to respect human rights and provides an account of those rights.[48] The fiduciary conception explicitly prohibits waste. There is a duty to protect and conserve what is common for others, including future generations.[49] John Locke argues that people should be accustomed "from their cradles to spoil or waste nothing at all."[50]

---

45. John Locke, "Second Treatise of Government," Peter G. Brown, *Restoring the Public Trust* (1994), 69.

46. John Locke, "Second Treatise," *The English Philosophers from Bacon to Mill*, ed. Edwin A Burtt, par. 7. Brown, 72.

47. Brown, 72; John Locke, Second Treatise, *The English Philosophers from Bacon to Mill*, ed. Edwin A. Burtt, par. 222.

48. Brown, 74.

49. Brown, 74.

50. John Locke, "Some Thoughts Concerning Education," as quoted in Richard Ashcraft, *Revolutionary Politics* and Locke's "Two Treatises of Government" (1986), 266.

GOVERNMENTAL SURVIVABILITY DERIVES FROM ITS INTEGRITY

Active application of the fiduciary model could transform American politics. A sense of fiduciary responsibility would prompt elected officials to a renewed sense of mission. At the same time, the people's perception of the fiduciary model would impact citizens with a fresh reason to expect integrity from their government and a deeper understanding of what they do when they vote.[51] The fiduciary conception captures the concept that governments and those who compose them have a responsibility to care for the governed.[52] Unavoidably, the governed and those governing are interdependent. Trust rests on the moral obligation between them.[53]

Trusteeship places concern for the well-being of citizens, especially the vulnerable, at the center of governmental responsibility.[54] The trustees' fundamental responsibility is to forestall harm between citizens.[55] In this vein, Peter Brown imports wisdom from the parable of the Good Samaritan. In protecting citizens, trustees are not to exhaust all resources, so that they are unable to carry on the other affairs of state. Neither are trustees to forgo their own journey—that is, abandon their agenda for the good of the country while they protect citizens.[56] In a trust model, all obligations of the fiduciaries to the voters are based on promises—and the promises of a fiduciary must be kept.[57]

Public fiduciaries should not feel isolated from those they serve, however. They should not see among the American people the "unproblematically independent Robinson Crusoe" as a major figure. Citizens generally are not like the independent Robinson Crusoe; therefore government should be alert to assist citizens.[58] The American people care about having objective, fair, and honest

51. Brown, 79.
52. Brown, 80.
53. Brown, 84.
54. Brown, 84–85.
55. Brown, 85.
56. Brown, 85.
57. Brown, 85.
58. Brown, 85.

authorities who allow them to express themselves, yet treat them with dignity and respect.[59]

The Present Need for Integrity-Fostering Devices

The present need, therefore, for integrity-fostering devices is legion. Integrity-fostering devices are essential in the aftermath of Watergate and Contragate. Although the lessons of both tragedies may be multiplied, one lesson of Iran/Contra is the need for internal oversight from within the executive complex. If an agency within the executive branch was created to investigate other agencies and report to the President, the aegis of ignorance would shrink, though not disappear. If a camouflaged junta within the executive complex had operatives systematically lie not only to Congressional oversight committees and but also to a co-executive investigative agency, the junta chameleon would more likely reveal its true color. The creation of an executive agency for internal self-regulation would be a step up from the slough of Iran/Contra. Presidential power projection, subject to in-house as well as Congressional oversight, might redeem its lost credibility. This addition to the palladia of federal checks and balances could materialize by executive order. The need for such an order is underscored by the poignant words of Justice Robert Jackson: "The rise of administrative bodies probably has been the most significant legal trend of the last half-century and perhaps more values are affected by their decisions than those of all the courts."[60]

Actually, a forerunner of such an internal review agency exists in the Special Review Board created by President Ronald Reagan on December 1, 1986, to investigate NSC operations. The three-personed bipartisan commission, led by John Tower, produced the Tower Board Report, which chronicled confused

---

59. Tom R. Tyler, *Why People Obey the Law* (New Haven, CT: Yale University Press, 1990).

60. Justice Robert H. Jackson, in FTC v. Ruberoid Co. (1952). James O. Freedman, *Crisis and Legitimacy: The Administrative Process and American Government* (1978).

lines of communication and breached accountability in failures to report to the President. A similar permanent review board could systematically sniff around the executive complex for administrative waste. By answering to the President rather than Congress, the internal review board could foster self-correction.

In the shadow of Watergate, Contragate, and Whitewater, cynicism abounds; integrity-fostering devices would help foster credibility. In the Judge Clarence Thomas hearings debacle, for instance, Joe Klein in *New York* magazine said "the judge was worse than unconvincing; he was an embarrassment, frightened, hollow, running away from his writings of the past ten years." The Senate committee required the nominee to articulate his constitutional philosophy. Ronald Dworkin wrote in *New York Review* that "Thomas flunked that test in a spectacular way."[61] Further, Jane Mansbridge's cynicism is advanced; she characterized American politicians as motivated solely by selfishness. As Mansbridge declaims: "Self-interest is distinct from the motivations of duty and love. Politics is merely an unfolding of self-interest."[62] In his insightful discussion of "Whither Theories of the State?" Carnoy perceives:

> Politics in the United States is now at center stage at the very moment that political participation seemed to have lost all momentum. The reason for this is clear: the world capitalist crisis, emerging from the tumultuous 1960s, heralds the decline of the welfare State—of the "solution" to the previous crisis, fifty years ago. But this time around, it is not only the economy's performance that is called into question, but also the State's.[63]

---

61. Paul Simon, *Advice and Consent* (1992), 152; 76 Calif. L. Rev. 939, 950–51.

62. Jane J. Mansbridge, *Beyond Self-Interest* (Chicago: University of Chicago, 1990); for an exploration of the relation of political "centers" and the duration of political leadership, see Henry Bienen and Nocolas Van De Walle, *Of Time and Power: Leadership Duration in the Modern World* (1991).

63. Martin Carnoy, *The State and Political Theory* (1984), 246.

THE NEXUS OF GOVERNMENTAL INTEGRITY AND THE SURVIVABILITY

With the advent of a new era since November 8, 1994, politics is even more at center stage. The American people have contracted for new demands of performance. The new Congressional regime is now called to prove its integrity—that is, keep its promises.

CREDIBILITY A GATEWAY TO LEGITIMACY

Credibility Defined as a Positive Social Consensus

Credibility is the degree the governed trust the governors. As Max Weber explains:

> The belief in the legitimacy of rule is a value judgment, and depending on our values we, as aggregates of citizens and organized groups like the military, are willing to believe in the right of a rule to give commands, to find obedience, to impose sanctions against those who want to overthrow him.[64]

In his chapter "Focus: The Function of a Center in a Search for the Authoritative," Vining incisively zeroes in on the center of the American legal complex.

> Most serious would be the loss of a center. Not in an apocalyptic sense, that the center would not hold and things would fall apart: the center of the legal system would continue to be the law. The center has never been the institutions producing over time the numerous texts from which the law is drawn. But—King, Pope, President, Governor, Allah, Jehovah, Buddha, Jove, Wotan—why is there so often only one set up to speak?

None in this esteemed list of lawmakers could rule effectively unless he were trusted. To be trusted, lawmakers must be credible.[65] Accordingly, Dworkin adds, "law's empire is defined by attitude,

---

64. Juan J. Linz, "Legitimacy of Democracy and the Socioeconomic System," in *Comparing Pluralist Democracies: Strains on Legitimacy* (Mattei Dogan ed. 1988), 65.

65. Joseph Vining, *The Authoritative and the Authoritarian* (1986), 77.

not territory or power or process."⁶⁶ For law to work, those under it must feel good about it; Dahl remarks that even those who lose cases may still feel good because their right to heard has not been violated. A day in court, even if one loses, has a salutary effect. Therefore, Thomas Pownall remarked, "you may exert power over, but you can never govern, an unwilling people."⁶⁷ Law is effective to the degree law controls. Walls and a door may control behavior only if people consent to the walls and door—they could tear them down. Consider Bosnia. Law controls, therefore, to the degree those who make, enforce, and interpret law are credible. The character of legitimacy derives from the beliefs and values of the governed, and its summum bonum is its ability to command obedience to the rulers.⁶⁸ A wide variety of regimes has earned legitimacy among the governed. Dahl observes that in "some time and place, almost every conceivable political arrangement—feudalism, monarchy, oligarchy, hereditary aristocracy, plutocracy, representative government, direct democracy—has acquired so much legitimacy that men have volunteered their lives in its defense."⁶⁹

For a representative democracy to maintain unity despite its diversity, representative democracy must nurture its credibility.⁷⁰ The adversary model of democracy presupposes the citizens' interests are in constant conflict. The unitary model of democracy presupposes the "consensual and common interest, effected by face-to-face relations and singularity of concern."⁷¹ According to either model, representative democracy can not survive without credibility. Oliver Wendell Holmes describes how experience more than logic has characterized the Legitimization of law.

66. Ronald D. Dworkin, *Law's Empire* (1986).

67. April 12, 1769, Jerrilyn Greene Marston, *King and Congress: The Transfer of Political Legitimacy* (1987), 3.

68. Cf. Max Weber, *The Theory of Social Organization* (New York, 1963) (1922).

69. Robert A. Dahl, *Modern Political Analysis* (3rd ed. 1976), 61 quoted by Jerrilyn Greene Marston, *King and Congress: The Transfer of Political Legitimacy* (1987), 3–4.

70. Jane J. Mansbridge, *Beyond Adversary Democracy* (1980), 3.

71. *Id.*

> The life of the law has not been logic, it has been experience. The felt necessities of the time, the prevalent moral and political theories, institutions of public policy, avowed or unconscious, even the prejudices which judges share with their fellow-men, have had a good deal more to do than the syllogism in determining the rules by which men should be governed.[72]

Accordingly, those governed by representative democracy learn to trust or doubt their government by experience more than logic.

Legitimization through Credibility Defined

The legitimacy of a social order is the effective belief in its binding or obligatory quality.[73] Merelman defines legitimacy as an empirical belief.

> [It is] belief that the structures, procedures, actions, decisions, policies of officials, or political leaders of the state possess the quality of rightness, or appropriateness, of the moral good, and ought to be recognized in virtue of this quality.[74]

Weber closely associates legitimacy with stability.

> Action, especially social action which involves a social relationship, may be guided by the belief in the existence of a legitimate order. The probability that action will actually be so governed will be called the validity (Geltung) of the order in question.[75]

---

72. Oliver W. Holmes, *The Common Law* (1945), 1.

73. Nisbett and Wilson, "Telling More Than We Can Know: Verbal Reports on Mental Processes," 84 Psychological Re. (1977), 231, 380–81, 398.

74. Merelman, "Learning and Legitimacy," 60 Am. Pol. Sci. Rev. (1966), 548.

75. Max Weber, *Economy and Society: An Outline of Interpretative Sociology* (G. Roth & C. Wittich eds. 1968), 381.

GOVERNMENTAL SURVIVABILITY DERIVES FROM ITS INTEGRITY

Two minimum conditions are necessary and sufficient for the existence of a legal system: rules that generally regulate behavior and the general acceptance of common public standards.[76] Every "system attempts to establish and to cultivate the belief in its legitimacy."[77] When a system has established its validity or *Geltung*, governmental decisions are generally obeyed without threat of sanctions. Nisbett and Wilson elaborate that governments viewed as valid are rarely challenged.

> [They are] generally obeyed or adhered to, without the concurrent or immediate exercise of force, without the likely imposition of sanctions, without the force of tradition or habit, even against the interests of those affected.[78]

To the degree the governed perceive the validity of a government, the governed willingly submit to that government.

Credibility Described as an Abstraction or Myth

Credibility among the governed develops into a unifying abstraction, a moral, quasireligious consensus. Hobbes implied the myth in his *Leviathan*: "Leviathan is set on his feet; he is the king of the proud; but his feet are clay; he too is a fiction."[79] Jane Rutherford illustrates the function of myth through her allusion to Robin Hood. He embodied the myth of the equitable redistribution of wealth.

> One man calleth me kind, another calleth me cruel; this one calleth me good, honest fellow, and that one vile thief. Truly, the world hath as many eyes to look upon a man withal as there are spots on a toad; so, with what pair of eyes thou regardest me lieth entirely with thine own self.[80]

---

76. Nisbett and Wilson, 231.

77. *Economy and Society* 213. Nisbett and Wilson, 398.

78. Nisbett and Wilson, 398.

79. p. xv. essay by W.F. Pogson Smith, "The Philosophy of Hobbes," introduction Thomas Hobbes, *Hobbes' Leviathan* (1929).

80. Howard Pyle, *The Merry Adventures of Robin Hood* (1883) (Dover

THE NEXUS OF GOVERNMENTAL INTEGRITY AND THE SURVIVABILITY

To the creative Rutherford, due process, like Robin Hood, is a myth. It is a set of stories, texts, and values that have been handed down through the years to regulate the relationships between people and government. The myth has always incorporated both procedural and substantive elements, and the unifying themes of due process have been a commitment to three central values: law, participation, and equality. These values affect the balance of power among individuals, communities, and government.[81] The Fourteenth Amendment, according to Rutherford, connects the Due Process Clause, the Privileges and Immunities Clause, and the Equal Protection Clause into "the dignity myth, utility myth, contract myth"[82] The myth of due process staves off the fear of arbitrary government.[83] The binding of force of the secular Constitution has come to hold an oracular semi-divine aura. The exegetical role of judges images the judicial role of Hebrew prophets.[84] To Rutherford, the American government has quasireligious dimensions.

Generally, myths are sacred traditions. They may be illusions, fables, or expressions of moral truths.[85] Myths are also the stories that are told to pass on cultural values. As myths are retold, they are often embellished. As a result, myths frequently combine fact and fantasy, and gradually change over time. "Myth is to be defined as a complex of stories—some no doubt fact, and some fantasy—which, for various reasons, human beings regard as demonstration of the inner meaning of the universe and of human life."[86] Myths are living creations of a culture, and viewed from within the culture, they represent core values that some also may view as central

---

Publications 1968), 160.

81. Jane Rutherford, "The Myth of Due Process," 72 B.U.L. (1992), Rev. 1, 4.

82. Rutherford, Rev. 1, 3.

83. Rutherford, Rev. 1, 7.

84. cf. Robert Burt, "Constitutional Law and the Teaching of the Parables," 93 Yale L.J. (1984), 455, 465. On a religious and moral plane, Martin Luther denied the legitimacy of the Papacy long before he burned a Papal imprimatur.

85. Geoffrey S. Kirk, *Myth: Its Meaning and Functions in Ancient and Other Cultures* (1970), 20–33; Rutherford, Rev. 1, 4.

86. Alan Watts, "Myth and Ritual in Christianity" 7 (1953), quoted in Rutherford, Rev. 1, 4.

truths. In this sense myths are eternal; they explain the past, present, and future. Indeed they create the very fabric of the culture, that which distinguishes one culture from another. Viewed from other cultures, myths are mere fables. Accordingly, the very word 'myth' embodies a paradox. Depending on one's vantage point, myths are simultaneously true and fictional.[87]

Social Illustrations of Legitimization

Social legitimacy "connotes a broad, empirically determined societal acceptance of the system."[88] Some indigenous social entities "bear all the earmarks of law, including 'secondary' rules of recognition, change, and adjudication"—components of a full-fledged legal system, according to H.L.A. Hart.[89] In these indigenous social systems, "normative principles will say how people are to behave. But . . . they will have implications about the proper design of institutions, about the assignment of rights and positions of authority, and about the procedures to be followed in making decisions."[90] Private governments impose sanctions from ridicule to threats of physical violence.[91]

Examples of private governments are legion: unions, self-regulating professional associations, fraternities and sororities, and religious organizations.[92] Illegal private governments include drug cartels, gangs, and other organized criminal groups. Assemblies of God, a religious private government, suspended the Rev. Jimmy Swaggart because of alleged ethical violations. Swaggart no longer

87. Rutherford, Rev. 1, 3.

88. David. D. Caron, "The Legitimacy of the Collective Authority of the Security Council," 87 A.J.I.L. 552, 559.

89. Marc Galanter and David Luban, "Poetic Justice: Punitive Damages and Legal Pluralism," 42 Am. U.L. Rev. 1393, 1400; H.L.A. Hart, *The Concept of Law* (1961), 91–96.

90. *Politics and Process: New Essays in Democratic Thought* (Geoffrey Brennan ed. & Loren E. Lomasky, 1989), 69.

91. Stewart Macaulay, "Private Government," in *Law and the Social Science* (Leon Lipson and Stanton Wheeler eds., 1986), 445, 447.

92. Macaulay, 446–49, 450.

considered the Assemblies of God a legitimate private government and rejected the ecclesiastical court's judgment.[93] Even guards in a prison complex may constitute a private government. One empirical study of 358 guards at five prisons in four states found an unwritten set of rules of private government. Most guards viewed inmate social protest of unfair staff treatment as outside their rights. Guards' acceptance of inmate protest was related to background variables, including educational level, employment, job satisfaction, and institutional authority over inmates.[94]

Jeanne Kirkpatrick observed at the conventions of the two political parties in 1972 an unwritten code for cliques composing the new bands of elite presidential advisors. According to Kirkpatrick, among the delegates at the two conventions of 1972, factions at both conventions emerged with distinctive traits associated with sex, political generation, candidate preference, and social structure—the "new Presidential elite."[95] Letty M. Russell argues that even social language establishes positions of domination and subordination in legitimizing authority.[96]

Management Illustrations of Legitimization

A theory of deterrence underlies a compliance approach to business ethics. This approach focuses on the threat of detection and

93. The Louisiana District Presbytery of the Assemblies of God sanctioned Swaggart by suspension of three months, on appeal; the Executive Presbytery of the church's General Council sanctioned Swaggart by a suspension of one year. "Final Decision Due in Swaggart Case," *New York Times*, Mar. 4, 1988, at A12; "Church Defrocks Swaggart for Rejecting Its Punishment," *New York. Times*, Apr. 9, 1988, at 1; see generally *America's Religious Heretics* (George H. Shriver ed., 1966) (an analysis of various Protestant heresy trials), 9–12.

94. John R. Hepburn, "The Erosion of Authority and the Perceived Legitimacy of Inmate Social Protest: A Study of Prison Guards," *Journal of Criminal Justice* 1984 Vol. 12(6): 579–90.

95. Jeanne Kirkpatrick, *The New Presidential Elite: Men and Women in National Politics* (1976).

96. Letty M. Russell, "Inclusive Language and Power," Religious Education 1985 Vol. 80(4): 582–602.

punishment to channel behavior in moral and legal directions. The deterrence theory presupposes that humankind is composed of rational self-interested maximizers. Rational self-interested maximizers respond to the personal cost/benefit analysis of their decisions, not the moral and legal legitimacy of their decisions. Tom Tyler, however, disagrees, arguing that in American culture people generally maintain a considerable inclination to obey the law. Obedience to particular laws, however, is affected by the individual's perception of the law's legitimacy.[97]

Based on Tyler's thesis, Paine argues for integrity as a governing business ethic. The task of the business ethicist in Paine's business model is to "define and give life to an organization's guiding cues, to create an environment that supports ethically sound behavior, and to instill a sense of shared accountability among employees." The need for obedience is built into the organizational life as a business conscience. This conscience is viewed not as an imposing constraint imposed by external authorities, but as a positive guiding inner light. Organizational ethics become a driving force of an enterprise, the informer of the decision-making process, and a means of self-definition of the organization.[98]

To implement an ethics strategy, according to Paine, companies develop codes of conduct specifying appropriate behavior, along with a system of incentives, audits, and controls. The implementation of the ethics strategy includes developing attitudes and decision-making processes.[99] NovaCare, Wetherill, and Martin Marietta are three examples of corporations that successfully implemented ethics strategies.

NovaCare's high turnover rate was symptomatic of a lack of common values and aspirations. A "huge disconnect" between management and employees resulted in the high turnover. NovaCare, however, did not develop a specific code of conduct but a statement of vision. The statement articulates a vision, purpose

97. Lynn Sharp Paine, "Managing for Organizational Integrity," *Harvard Business Review*, March 1994.
98. Paine.
99. Paine.

and belief system. The purpose was meeting the rehabilitation needs of patients through clinical leadership as per four core beliefs: respect for the individual, service to the customer, pursuit of excellence, and commitment to personal integrity. Each belief is explained not only theoretically but also as it is manifested in day-to-day activities.[100]

Wetherill Associates uses the same integrity theory but does not have a conventional code of conduct or a statement of values. Wetherill has a Quality Assurance Manual, a combination of philosophy text, conduct guide, technical manual, and company profile. The company articulates its commitment to honesty and right action. Right action includes behavior that is logically, expediently, and morally right. All new recruits are indoctrinated that absolute honesty, mutual courtesy and respect are standard operating procedures.[101]

Martin Marietta implemented a company-wide management initiative aimed at creating and maintaining a "do-it-right" climate. A corporate ethics office manages a program to train personnel in a code of conduct, ethics, procedures for reporting and investigating ethical concerns, and a system for reporting violations of federal procurement law to the government. A steering committee, composed of the president, senior executives, and two rotating members selected from field operations, oversees the ethics office. An audit and ethics committee of the board of directors oversees the steering committee. On several occasions, Martin Marietta has voluntarily confessed and made restitution to the government for possible violations of federal procurement laws.[102]

---

100. Paine.

101. Paine; Catherine Smith B., "Do Legitimacy of Supervisor and Reward Contingency Interact in Prediction of Work Behavior?" *Human Relations* 1984 Dec Vol. 37(12), 1029–46.

102. Lynn Sharp Paine, "Managing for Organizational Integrity," *Harvard Business Review*, March 1994.

GOVERNMENTAL SURVIVABILITY DERIVES FROM ITS INTEGRITY

Military Illustrations of Legitimization

The explicit acceptance or denial of the legitimacy and authority of the police and army has little to do with coercive power.[103] Those who submit generally do so on their own accord. Conversely, in 1975, the political officer, another officer, and ten sailors aboard the Soviet Destroyer Storozhevoi mutinied. They surrendered only after being bombed by Soviet aircraft only 50 miles from Swedish territorial waters. The mutineers, led by Captain Third Rank V. Sablin, decided that the authority over them was power projected by an illegitimate regime. To be sure, the mutineers may have sought Western luxury and liberty, but their act derived from the negation of a political belief. Their political belief nullified the authority binding them.[104]

For military intervention, Caron underscores that a consensus is imperative for United Nations police actions to be legitimate.[105] To establish a new government of rebellious gladiators, Spartacus underscored his personal integrity as grounds to legitimate the slave army.

> Ye call me chief, and ye do well to call him chief who, for twelve long years, has met upon the arena every shape of man or beast that the broad Empire of Rome could furnish, and has never yet lowered his arm. And if there be one among you who can say that, ever, in public fight or private brawl, my actions did belie my tongue, let him step forth and say it. If there be three in all your throng dare face me on the bloody sand, let them come on![106]

---

103. Timo Airaksinen, "Coercion, Deterrence, and Authority," Theory & Decision 1984 Sep Vol. 17(2), 105–117.

104. A. Shalnev, "Was There a Mutiny on a Soviet Destroyer?" The Current Digest of the Soviet Press, *Foreign Affairs,* Volume XLII, No. 9, 25, citing Izvestia, Feb. 27, 6.

105. David. D. Caron, "The Legitimacy of the Collective Authority of the Security Council," 87 A.J.I.L. 552, 587–88.

106. Elijah Kellogg, "Spartacus to the Gladiators." Wilmot B. Mitchell, *Elijah Kellogg: The Man and His Work* (1903), 206.

THE NEXUS OF GOVERNMENTAL INTEGRITY AND THE SURVIVABILITY

Spartacus' unilateral leadership effected a consensus among the gladiators; and this consensus became the genesis of a new government.

In sum, in social relationships, business, religion, and military units, an authority structure's legitimization is imperative to maintain unity among the governed. Otherwise, disintegration occurs. Failure of a government, public or private, to legitimize means failure to survive. Sheep without a shepherd scatter.

DOMESTIC TRANQUILITY A GATEWAY TO ECONOMIC EFFICIENCY

Governments that promote Pareto optimality tend to legitimate themselves. Tragically, wars have a way of making the loser economically dead. Generally even a war's victor cannot suffer some loss to its Gross National Product. The best means to Pareto optimality is domestic tranquility.[107] Peace provides a forum to cultivate productivity.

Further, economic efficiency and contentment are related. General economic efficiency implies that individuals are fulfilling their potential by personal productivity. A consensus of psychologists holds that self-actualization includes personal productivity. Accordingly, personal productivity is generally a necessary means to the "pursuit of happiness." As Locke argues:

> God gave the world to men in common; but since He gave it them for their benefit, and the greatest conveniences of life they were able to draw from it, it cannot be supposed He meant it should always remain common and uncultivated. He gave it to the use of the industrious and rational (and labor was to be his title to it), not

---

107. For a concise discussion of Pareto optimality, see "Pareto Optimality, External Costs, and Income Redistribution" in James M. Buchanan and Gordon Tullock, *The Calculus of Consent: Logical Foundations of Constitutional Democracy* (1st ed. 1962) (1965), 188–99; *cf.* Juan J. Linz' discussion of the relation to legitimacy and economic efficiency in "Legitimacy of Democracy and the Socioeconomic System," in *Comparing Pluralist Democracies: Strains on Legitimacy* (Mattei Dogan ed. 1988), 81–85.

GOVERNMENTAL SURVIVABILITY DERIVES FROM ITS INTEGRITY

to the fancy or covetousness or the quarrelsome and contentious.

Locke's vision of efficiency, productivity, and domestic tranquility presupposes the individual's inviolable right to private property. As Charles Beard comments, "fundamental private rights of property are anterior to government and morally beyond the reach of popular majorities."[108] Civil wrongs that disturb social tranquility similarly wound economic efficiency. Punitive damages as a corrective to civil wrongs, in Galanter's view, are "merely an augmentation of compensatory damages to produce optimal economic efficiency."[109] Civil litigation, therefore, is a means to mend social rifts and restore optimal efficiency.[110]

CONCLUSION: THE ESSENTIAL LINKS IN THE POLITICAL CHAIN HOLDING TOGETHER A CONSTITUTIONAL REPUBLIC

The Essential Links in the Chain: Integrity, Credibility, Legitimacy, Tranquility, and Efficiency

Governments can not govern without a consensus of legitimacy among the governed. Legitimacy among the governed is proportioned to the credibility of those governing. The credibility of those governing is proportioned to their integrity. Integrity-fostering devices in government bolster the foundations of republican

---

108. Charles Beard, *An Economic Interpretation of the Constitution of the United States* (1936), 324.

109. Marc Galanter and David Luban, "Poetic Justice: Punitive Damages and Legal Pluralism," 42 Am. U.L. Rev. (1993), 1393, 1449.

110. The economic deterrence theory, however, fails in its application to criminal law, because the theory presupposes that "would-be criminals" rationally weigh costs and benefits of criminal activity. Gary S. Becker, "Crime and Punishment: An Economic Approach," 76 J. Pol. Econ. (1968), 169, 176–90.

Richard Posner points out that criminal sanctions are useful from an economic standpoint to impose additional costs on conduct where the conventional damages remedy would be insufficient to limit that conduct to the efficient level. Richard Posner, *Economic Analysis of Law* (2d ed. 1977), 163–64.

democracy because people's attitudes toward the law are influenced by normative judgments—their sense of what is right and wrong.[111]

Representative Democracy, Verity, and Survivability

Since Plato's *Euthyphro*, the question of whether there are eternal verities that even no divine will can alter has recurred in every age of philosophy.[112] Although discussion as to the existence, knowability, and nature of eternal verity continues, integrity as a principle of constitutional government is imperative. Constitutional democracy can not survive without the integrity of its functionaries. Some view the mechanics of American representative democracy with consternation—concern that "in the confusing world of due process of law, anything goes."[113] Although eternal verities may elude the policy analyst's grasp, the policy analyst must see integrity as an essential element of a representative democracy's Legitimization. If the "great experiment" of American constitutional democracy survives in this land, one need look no further for the reason than the ancient cry of Jewish prophets, "integrity springs up in the land."

---

111. Tom R. Tyler, *Why People Obey the Law* (New Haven, CT.: Yale University Press, 1990).

112. Patrick Riley, *Will and Political Legitimacy: A Critical Exposition of Social Contract Theory in Hobbes, Locke, Rousseau, Kant, and Hegel* (1982), at ix.

113. Eugene Hickok and Gary McDowell, *Justice and Law* (1993), 121.

MAJOR CASE IN POINT

The Fragmentation of Gorbachev's Government

INTRODUCTION

Former Soviet leader Mikhail Gorbachev, having assured himself a place in history with the laudatory title "transitional figure," remains paradoxical, if not enigmatic, to pundits.[1] Was he the pivotal figure whose policies triggered the mechanism of dismantling of a federal bureaucracy? Or, was he merely a catalyst for the process of the fragmentation of Soviet federalism already occurring? Matlock sees Gorbachev as a Moses who led the Russian people out of bondage but not quite to the Promised Land.[2] Gorbachev began his presidency in the confines of the cage of a chasm between what the Soviet system claimed to be and what it was.[3] Ironically, the removal of Gorbachev from the cage of this chasm eliminated it; the Soviet Union no longer exists. A

---

1. Robert G. Kaiser, "Gorbachev: Triumph and Failure," *Foreign Affairs* (Spring 1991), 160.

2. *Kirkus Reviews*, The Kirkus Service, Inc., September 1, 1995; Jack F. Matlock, *Autopsy on an Empire: Observing the Collapse of the Soviet Union* (Random, 1995) (writing after having left Moscow one week before the attempted coup, having served as U.S. ambassador to the USSR from 1987 to 1991).

3. Robert G. Kaiser, "Gorbachev: Triumph and Failure," *Foreign Affairs* (Spring 1991), 160.

hero appeared; expectations arose. A hero disappeared; an empire expired.[4]

STATEMENT OF THESIS

Prognosticators during Gorbachev's meteoric flash across the Russian sky and post-mortems thereafter tend to agree that Gorbachev's *Gesamtkonzept* (Comprehensive Concept) could not have worked. Truly, as Gary Hart quipped in 1991, "the reasons to bet against Gorbachev far outweigh those to bet for him."[5] In retrospect, Gorbachev's reforms, rather than stratify the Soviet federal crackled shell, accelerated its fragmentation. The Soviet federal monolith's failed integrity eroded social credibility. And so the domino progression advanced; loss of social credibility resulted in loss of political legitimacy. Loss of political legitimacy compromised governmental survivability.

GORBACHEV'S PRESIDENCY GOVERNED A SYSTEM ALREADY FRAGMENTING: HOW IT TEETERED ON COLLAPSE

The system that Mikhail Gorbachev inherited was a diversity of cultures and peoples held together by a martial wand. Relaxation of the reigns of force released divergent forces latent in the system, brewing beneath its superstructure. Gorbachev's *Perestroika* and *Glasnost* triggered the forces upward and outward.

---

4. Mark Frankland, *The Sixth Continent* (New York: Harper & Row, 1987), 158ff.

5. Gary Hart, *Russia Shakes the World: The Second Russian Revolution and Its Impact on the West* (New York: Cornelia & Michael Bessie Books, 1991), 223.

MAJOR CASE IN POINT

The Vulnerability of the Monolith

The pyramid structure of authority of the now-defunct Soviet Union was monolithic, a top-down bureaucracy, its power flowing only down. Authority in government derives from a sense of legitimacy, and the erosion of the monolith's perceived legitimacy had reached crisis proportions. Economically imperiled and structurally flawed because of its lack of checks and balances, the leviathan cringed in a death throe. Further, the perceived external threat—a historic reason to justify a centralized military command structure—diminished to the point that the governed wondered whether the megalithic center had outlived its usefulness.

Vulnerability Because of Its Structural Flaw: Absence of Checks and Balances

The Soviet system, partially because of its raw power without checks or balances, had largely lost credibility with those it governed. At the core of the legitimacy of any political system is the dynamic of how power is derived and distributed within it.[6] If the governed view power dynamics as fundamentally fair, the system's perceived legitimacy turns to credibility with the governed. Authority is "the power of legitimacy—the special power of a leader whom others obey because they view his commands as legitimate."[7] As Zbigniew Brzezinski noted, in the Soviet power apparatus "division of power means the sharing of a single resource: control over the Party organization . . ."[8] In the Leninist construct, the Party is power; but the reaction to Leninism was a repulsive sense of illegitimacy.

Undercurrents of belief, however, among the Soviet peoples under the weight of the Party hierarchy sounded not unlike the early currents of politicking that culminated in the Federalist

---

6. Thane Gustafson and Dawn Mann, "Gorbachev's First Year: Building Power and Authority," *Problems of Communism* (May–June 1986), 1.

7. Gustafson and Mann, 11.

8. Gustafson and Mann, 1.

papers.⁹ By a crude process of elimination, the political mood shifted toward a rule of law. As Soviet analyst Anatoly Sobchak concluded, the rule of law is based on the principle of the separation of powers, "whereas the basic principle of government by soviets as espoused by Lenin is that all of these elements be in one place."¹⁰ The Soviet peoples, however, had concluded that human nature, if allowed to proceed without restraint, would engender abuse and oppression.¹¹ Accumulation of the executive, legislative, and judiciary powers into the hands of one individual or one agency is the "very definition of tyranny."¹² Like Alexander Hamilton, the Soviet peoples desired a judiciary with "neither force nor will but merely judgment."¹³ Separation of powers, under rule of law, became a distant light at the end of the political tunnel for at least some of the population as they imbibed Western ideas.

Eventually, after the coup, the new Russian Federation would enter that light, at least on paper, providing in their Constitution:

> State power in the Russian Federation shall be exercised on the basis of its separation into legislative, executive and judicial branches. The bodies of legislative, executive and judicial branches shall be independent of each other.¹⁴

---

9. Bernard H. Siegan, *Drafting a Constitution for a Nation or Republic Emerging into Freedom* (1994), 14–16 (demonstrating that both parliamentary and American democracies maintain the separation of powers doctrine).

10. Anatoly Sobchak, "Uniting Political and Economic Reform," in *After Perestroika: Democracy in the Soviet Union*, Brad Roberts and Nina Belyaeva, eds. (Washington, D.C.: The Center for Strategic and International Studies, 1991), 63.

11. *The Federalist* No. 51 (James Madison), reprinted in *Classic Readings in American Politics* (Pietro S. Nivola & David H. Rosenblum eds., 1986), 49.

12. *The Federalist* No. 47 (James Madison), reprinted in *Classic Readings*, 43–44.

13. *The Federalist* No. 78 (Alexander Hamilton) reprinted in *Classic Readings*, 514.

14. Russian Constitution article 10.

MAJOR CASE IN POINT

Vulnerability Because of a Minimized External Threat

Although the West saw the Soviet system as monolithic, indestructible, perhaps even destined to "bury us,"[15] Jack Matlock, in his seminal *Autopsy on an Empire: Observing the Collapse of the Soviet Union*, believes that the fundamental reason for the Soviet Union's collapse was "the coincidence of a Western policy that combined strength and a willingness to negotiate fairly, with a Soviet leadership that realized that it had to change."[16] Matlock believes the United States and other democratic countries were "major factors" in bringing about the end of Soviet communism, "as a result not so much of their policies but of their very existence."[17]

Further, the Soviet Union and the United States no longer had very different concepts of detente.[18] The Soviet concept of foreign policy had evolved—the "nuclear sufficiency" doctrine averted the Clausewitz dogma, which conceivably could include a first strike.[19] As Tsuyoshi Hasegawa exposited the New Soviet foreign policy:

> Clausewitz's classical formula has become hopelessly obsolete. It belongs to libraries. To place all-human, moral-ethical norms in the foundation of international politics and to humanize interstate relations has for the first time in history become a vital requirement.[20]

15. "Commentary: In the Final Act of the Drama, Gorbachev Gets the Hook," *The Washington Times*, December 22, 1991.

16. *Kirkus Reviews*, The Kirkus Service, Inc., September 1, 1995; Jack F. Matlock, *Autopsy on an Empire: Observing the Collapse of the Soviet Union* (Random, 1995) (writing after having the left Moscow one week before the attempted coup, having served as U.S. ambassador to the USSR from 1987 to 1991).

17. *Kirkus Reviews*, The Kirkus Service, Inc., September 1, 1995.

18. David Holloway, "Gorbachev's New Thinking," *Foreign Affairs* 68 (1988/89), 67.

19. Serweryn Bialer, "'New Thinking' and Soviet Foreign Policy," *Survival* (July/August, 1988), 291ff.

20. Tsuyoshi Hasegawa, "Gorbachev, The New Thinking of Soviet Foreign-Security Policy and the Military: Recent Trends ad Implications," Peter Juviler and Hiroshi Kimura, eds. *Gorbachev's Reforms: U.S. and Japanese*

THE NEXUS OF GOVERNMENTAL INTEGRITY AND THE SURVIVABILITY

Contrary to a generation claiming that NATO was "poised to attack" the USSR, the Soviet peoples had largely concluded that claim was a propagandistic caprice.[21]

Vulnerability Because of Its Economic Plight

Hindsight demonstrates the accuracy of Gorbachev's view that the Soviet interior was a crackled fragile shell, awaiting an economic *Perestroika* or collapse.[22] The stalled economy of the monolith had become a lethal political cancer. As Alexander Rutskoi, Vice President to Gorbachev successor Boris Yeltsin, expressed the common bond of desperation: "Either we shall live like the rest of the world, or we shall continue to call ourselves the 'Socialist Choice' and 'the Communist Prospect' and live like pigs."[23] In the same desperate vein, Yeltsin opined to the Soviet Parliament on November 20, 1991: "It is our last chance, we must make Russia and all the republics work." At the same time, the beleaguered Gorbachev appealed to the Soviet Parliament for more republic money for the central coffers. He projected for 1992 a nine percent fall in agricultural production, seven percent drop in industrial production, thirty-one percent decline in exports and a forty-two percent fall in imports. Yeltsin's tone, however, at the same meeting was more involved with keeping his people alive; he argued that there were sufficient supplies of flour and "there will not be a famine."[24] Starving people do not make good vassals; rather, they make good revolutionaries. Gorbachev's inherited system, because

---

Assessments (New York: Aldine De Gruyter, 1988), 119.

21. Conversely, from the West's military perspective, the decomposing Soviet infrastructure cooled its militaristic rhetoric. Domestic decomposition is a powerful cooler of martial ardor.

22. Commentary, "In the Final Act of the Drama, Gorbachev Gets the Hook," *The Washington Times*, December 22, 1991.

23. Michael Mandelbaum, "Coup de Grace: The End of the Soviet Union," *Foreign Affairs* 71 (1991/92), 181–82.

24. Mary Dejevsky, "Yeltsin Appoints 'Last Chance' Team," *The Times*, November 21, 1991.

MAJOR CASE IN POINT

of its stalled economy, monolithic power structure, and minimized sense of external threat, seemed unable to stand.

The Complex of Diverging Forces in Motion

The perversity of Gorbachev's law, "if it ain't broke, it soon will be," became Gorbachev's legacy. Sisyphus had one burden to lift; Gorbachev seemed to be a magnet for one catastrophe after another. Chernobyl exploded. Colossal earthquakes shook Armenia. Massive droughts and premature cold gutted the wheat harvest. The world price of oil dropped dramatically. Imports plummeted. Debts multiplied. Historians tend to ignore that Gorbachev was just plain unlucky.

Ironically, the manifold forces of change, divergent as they were, converged to eventually depose the bright new reformer. Never at ease in what he called the myriad "fields of tension,"[25] Gorbachev whirled in a diversity including conservatives unprepared for change and ultra-leftists who wanted to jump ahead too quickly. Gorbachev, the tactician, maneuvered himself into the vortex, attempting to ameliorate the antipodes. But leading from the center presupposes a congealed center exists; the political center was a maelstrom which flushed him out of office. The whirlpool of forces for change included economic stagnation, reactionary conservatism, resurgent nationalism, political liberalism, and an even an awakened sense of history and its lessons.

Economic Stagnation

Soviet consumers were more concerned about goods than Communism. The economic blight worsening, consumerism and Communism grew in inverse proportion. Had Gorbachev followed the Chinese example of revitalizing the consumer goods sector, he may have allayed the ever-enlarging desperation.[26] Gorbachev's

25. Mikhail Gorbachev, "How We See the World Today," *Perestroika*, 121.
26. Marshal I. Goldman, "Gorbachev the Economist," *Foreign Affairs* 69

attempt to alleviate the lack of consumer products through super-ministries, such as the *Gospriemka*, a quality control group of inspectors, actually aggravated consumer dissatisfaction. "The center," through its agency *Gospriemka*, increased its control over day-to-day operations to Khrushchev and Brezhnev levels.[27] The Stalinist simplicity gone—taxes, expenditures, monetary policy, interest rates, supply and demand, and competition controlled by a wave of the imperial wand—the economic complexity of *Perestroika* enraveled Gorbachev and his economic advisors.[28]

Further, conflicting legal signals frustrated the noble purpose of *Perestroika*. On July 1, 1986, for instance, "unearned income" from the sale of products produced by somebody else was banned. Schizophrenically, on May 1, 1987, establishment of individual, family, and cooperative businesses became legal. The restriction of the interchange of goods paralyzed the newly legalized businesses. Stymied by one legislation while buoyed by another, the growing entrepreneurial class became disgusted.[29] Ill-advised, misguided, and even self-contradictory policies engendered a curious consensus — the head of the mutating economic organism was no longer needed. The sprightly new capitalist class, bred by *Perestroika*, turned on their creator because they believed the umbilical cord from the center, although no longer wrapped around their necks, was wrapped around their wallets. The Gordian knot of the command economy engendered *Perestroika* to unravel it, but *Perestroika* convinced the Soviet peoples to cut the whole megalith.

Lenin's oft-repeated slogan, "Communism equals Soviet power plus electrification of the whole country," became a nauseating cliche, not only because of bureaucratic red tape, but also bureaucratic corruption.[30] *Perestroika* actually magnified bureau-

---

(1990), 33.

27. Goldman, p. 34.

28. Marshall I. Goldman, *What Went Wrong with Perestroika* (New York: W.W. Norton, 1991), 128.

29. Goldman, *What Went Wrong*, 34.

30. Geoffrey Hosking, *The Awakening of the Soviet Union* (Cambridge: Harvard University Press, 1990), 50.

MAJOR CASE IN POINT

cratic corruption: ". . . they cast their communist past overboard and became, overnight, enthusiastic 'marketers.'"[31] *Perestroika* enabled government bureaucrats of all ranks, first, to launder their ill-gotten wealth, second, to plunder openly, more widely, and with impunity, and third, to urge people to write off the promises offered them by the old regime. Moreover, increased government corruption and debt, both incurred and owed, complicated the stagnation. The problems of debt incursion and remittance added yet more strata to the confusion. As of November 1, 1989, for instance, state accountants claimed that developing debtor countries owed the Soviet Union $67 billion.[32] In sum, the Soviet economy had evolved into a state of near extinction.

Reactionary Conservatism

Even the conservatives admitted the need for change, but they confined their purview to the need to remove "Stalinist accretions." Even Soviet Premier Nikita Khruschev, who preceded Gorbachev by twenty years, called Stalinism "the boil on the healthy body of Soviet socialism."[33] Although *Perestroika* would open a Pandora's box of price increases, unemployment, and class inequality—evils which Marxist propagandists loved to hate[34]—the conservatives' message ("What's evil about the system is Stalinism. Get rid of that and we have the best system, better than Western capitalism") fell on unsympathetic ears.

Aggravating disaffection with the conservative hierarchy, the top tier of the conservative-controlled caste was not comprised of the best and brightest of the population. Rather, the system did

---

31. Sergei Yakovlev, *The Strannik*, Federal Information Systems Corporation, Official Kremlin International News Broadcast, March 23, 1993.

32. C.R. Neu, *Soviet International Finance in the Gorbachev Era* (Santa Monica: Rand Corp., 1991), x.

33. Serweryn Bialer, "The Death of Soviet Communism," *Foreign Affairs* 70 (1991/92), 171.

34. Marshall I. Goldman, *What Went Wrong with Perestroika* (New York: W.W. Norton, 1991), 125.

not encourage initiative, imagination, or decisiveness but rather rewarded dull conformity and slavish submission to the feudal power structure.[35] Even *Pravda* in 1986, echoing Milovan Djilas' *The New Class*, condemned the "entrenched, inert, immovable bureaucratic party," replete with privileges, separated from the working people.[36] But the bright, quick, personally adaptable, dynamic, and courageous Gorbachev was hardly the Party stereotype.[37] Hard-core party fundamentalists, who held Marxist-Leninist doctrine and "official" history inviolate, opposed Gorbachev as a heretic, or at least a compromiser.[38] Reactionaries viewed Gorbachev's liberalism and charisma as a threat to their positions.

According to Yeltsin, for instance, stalling *Perestroika* more than any other was the reactionary intriguer Ligachev. Adhering to the old style of leadership, he compiled secret dossiers, as tools for "McCarthyish" slander, as well as sabotaged goods distribution to foment consumer disaffection.[39] The Nineteenth Party Conference, held June 28, 1988, was a milestone in the evaluation of the pros and cons of *Perestroika*. There Ligachev, clinging to the Brezhnevian past, stated, "When people ask me where I was then, my answer is: I was in Tomsk and I was building Socialism."[40] Ligachev claimed that economic problems were temporary and remediable, and so exhorted his comrades, "We had both hard frosts

---

35. Michael Mandelbaum, "Coup de Grace: The End of the Soviet Union," *Foreign Affairs* 71 (1991/92), 166.

36. E. Doder, *Shadows and Whispers: Power Politics Inside the Kremlin from Brezhnev to Gorbachev* (New York: Random House, 1986). Party *apparatchiks*, for instance, opposed what they thought was hot air at the Central Committee plenum of January 1987; any agenda giving the Party a secondary role in a restructured state was heresy. Robert G. Kaiser, "Gorbachev: Triumph and Failure," *Foreign Affairs* 70 (Spring 1991), 162.

37. Serweryn Bialer, "The Death of Soviet Communism," *Foreign Affairs*, 171.

38. Baruch A. Hazan, *Gorbachev and His Enemies: The Struggle for Perestroika* (Boulder: Westview Press, 1990), 294–95.

39. Seweryn Bialer, "The Yeltsin Affair," *Politics, Society, and Nationality Inside Gorbachev's Russia* (Boulder: Westview Press, 1992), 94–95.

40. *Pravda*, July 2, 1988, 11.

MAJOR CASE IN POINT

and thaws, but what we need is simply stable good weather."[41] When Cheney, for instance, talked in 1989 of a possible "fall of Gorbachev" by old-liners who were likely to oust him,[42] he probably had Ligachev, among others, in mind.

The political alliances the hard-liners formed, however, belied ideological bankruptcy. The "Soyuz" faction, an alliance of Communists and military personnel, urged an emergency crackdown on the democrats but appeared unconcerned about reimposition of Communist ideological orthodoxy. Walter Ruby of *The Jerusalem Post*, for instance, was aghast when Soyuz leader Victor Alksnis actually appealed to Gorbachev to declare martial law and outlaw all political parties, even the Communist party. But, the Soyuz faction was apparently unaware that even elite units, morally rehabilitated from bygone Stalinist heartlessness, would not shoot at Russians or their slavic brothers.[43] More telling is the noisy silence, for instance, of the putsch about Marxist-Leninist ideology; in their martial law declaration, they struck "Communism" and "the Party" from their testimony.[44] Although Gorbachev took up the task of chiseling away at "Stalinist accretions,"[45] he instead struck a network of fissures so deep the entire monolith fell to pieces.

Resurgent Nationalism

In light of the resurgent nationalism under the Soviet hegemony, Gorbachev's task of pleasing both captive and captor was Herculean.[46] Robert Kaiser saw nationalism and free speech as a

41. Thane Gustafson and Dawn Mann, "Gorbachev's First Year: Building Power and Authority," *Problems of Communism* (May–June 1986), 11.

42. John M. Broder, "Prospects for Gorbachev Reforms? Cheney Backpedals Slightly," *Los Angeles Times*, May 4, 1989.

43. Serweryn Bialer, "The Death of Soviet Communism," *Foreign Affairs* 70 (1991/92), 178.

44. Bialer, *Foreign Affairs*, 175.

45. Michael Mandelbaum, "Coup de Grace: The End of the Soviet Union," *Foreign Affairs* 71 (1991/92), 169.

46. Robert G. Kaiser, "Gorbachev: Triumph and Failure," *Foreign Affairs* 70 (Spring 1991), 164.

death knell for the Soviet federalism: "Once Latvians, Ukrainians, Moldavians, Armenians and all the others felt free to speak their minds, organize politically and express their aspirations, the days of the old union were numbered."[47] The conjured genie could not be distilled back into the bottle; speech and assembly are forces that, once galvanized, do not break. In Gorbachev's case, he discovered he could not bend them, either.

The fervor for national identity in the republics was deep. George S.N. Luckyj, for instance, saw the literature of the republics in the late 1960s and early 1970s as a matter of national self-expression.[48] At the same time, Communism, both doctrine and heritage, was repulsive to many, if not most, non-Russian citizens of the USSR.[49] A stronger communal consciousness among Soviet Jews developed in the wake of *numerus clausus* and cadres policy, fueling both Zionism and more rigid religious observance.[50] Calls came from the Soviet media to allow for diversity: "We must treat diversity normally, as the natural state of the world; not with clenched teeth, as in the past, but normally as an immutable feature of social life."[51] Even Yeltsin, son of a Siberian peasant, opined that Muscovites do not hide their "snobbery and arrogance" toward provincials.[52] Nationalist forces, catalyzed to a fervor through *Glasnost*, were too strong to contain.

47. Kaiser, p. 169.

48. George S. N. Luckyj, *Discordant Voices: The Non-Russian Soviet Literatures* (Oakville, Ont.: Mosaic Press, 1975), 139–40; Maurice Friedberg, *Russian Culture in the 1980s* (Washington, D.C.: Center for Strategic and International Studies, 1985), 42.

49. Kaiser, 164.

50. Laurie P. Salitan, "Politics and Nationality," *Politics, Society, and Nationality Inside Gorbachev's Russia*. Seweryn Bialer, ed. (Boulder: Westview Press, 1982), 176.

51. *Izvestiya*, October 28, 1986.

52. Leon Aron, "Yeltsin: Russia's Rogue Populist: Is Gorbachev's Maverick Nemesis Poised to Profit from Bad Times?" *The Washington Post*, June 3, 1990.

MAJOR CASE IN POINT

Political Liberalism

Political liberalism under Gorbachev, allowing for new free speech freedoms, granted much in the public square; but the public square eventually colluded to exterminate the potential oppressor. The Pandora's box of tolerance bred a diverse litter, united only by their intolerance of intolerance. The foci of the political liberalism were *Glasnost* and democratization.

Ideas rule people, and *Glasnost* was the means of freely disseminating ideas. Suspecting another propagandistic caprice,[53] the Soviet populace looked for the proof of *Perestroika* in its pudding. *Glasnost* allowed open critical review of *perestroika's* dynamics. The newspapers were filled with discussion: ". . . the media have been filled with so many conflicting opinions about so many subjects it is unlikely anyone will ever again imagine that the Soviet system or its people are somehow 'monolithic.'"[54] Perhaps only one consensus had already developed, a belief that Marxist-Leninism's claim to scientific status was a fraud, the Communist party's claim to integrity in leadership a lie, and "the center" had to be decapitated.[55]

To Hauslohner, understanding of the evolution of *Perestroika* demands apprehension of

> the important rule change since Stalin—the cessation, then delegitimization, of the use of physical violence against otherwise loyal political opponents and of terror against potential counterelites and other suspect groups in the population.[56]

---

53. Tatsuo Kaneda, "Gorbachev's Economic Reforms," in *Gorbachev's Reforms: U..S. and Japanese Assessments*. Peter Juviler and Hiroshi Kimura, eds. (New York: Aldine De Gruyter, 1988), 81–82.

54. Yegor Yakovlev, "Flagship of Glasnost," in *Voices of Glasnost: Interviews with Gorbachev's Reformers* (New York: W. W. Norton, 1989), 197.

55. Michael Mandelbaum, "Coup de Grace: The End of the Soviet Union," 166.

56. Peter Hauslohner, "Politics before Gorbachev: De-Stalinization and the Roots of Reform," in *Politics, Society, and Nationality Inside Gorbachev's Russia* (Boulder: Westview Press, 1982), 47.

THE NEXUS OF GOVERNMENTAL INTEGRITY AND THE SURVIVABILITY

Gorbachev quoted Victor Hugo in his speech to the Council of Europe, Strasbourg, July 6, 1989, "A day will come when markets, open to trade, and minds, open to ideas, will become the sole battlefields." But Gorbachev brought the day; formal debate even emerged on official state television programming.[57] *Izvestiya* urged toleration: "we must get used to the idea that a multiplicity of voices is a natural part of openness."[58] Most significant to the development was the making and remaking of an outspoken Soviet intelligentsia.[59]

Further, *Glasnost* brought a new self-awareness. The confession of Eduard Shevardnadze, for instance, concerning sins of the evil empire "was less remarkable for its substance—which was well known anyway—than for its style." The new style fit a planned trip to the Vatican and a new "peace offensive" to the United States and Western Europe. It did not fit as well the Soviets' continuing shipments of money and weapons into the Western Hemisphere.[60] As the Soviet invasion of Afghanistan in December 1979 marked the end of the period of rapid Soviet expansion after the fall of Saigon, the brutality and cynicism of the invasion shocked the world. In an extraordinary *mea culpa* in the winter of 1989 Foreign Minister Eduard Shevardnadze admitted that the invasion had "violated civilized norms."[61]

Additionally, the environmental crisis exacerbated the popular discontent. The Ministry of Health added insult to injury to the women and children fleeing Chernobyl, stating "there is science without victims."[62] Minister of Health Evgenii Chasov reported in

57. Gail W. Lapidus, "State and Society," *Politics, Society, and Nationality Inside Gorbachev's Russia* (Boulder: Westview Press, 1982), 133.

58. *Izvestiya*, October 28, 1986.

59. Moshe Lewin, *The Gorbachev Phenomenon: A Historical Interpretation* (Berkeley: University of California Press, 1988), 48.

60. Gary Hart, *Russia Shakes the World: The Second Russian Revolution and Its Impact on the West* (New York: Cornelia & Michael Bessie Books, 1991), 75.

61. Hart, 180.

62. Jonathon Eisen, ed. *The Glasnost Reader* (New York: Penguin Books, 1990), 273.

MAJOR CASE IN POINT

1989 that 70 million people in 103 cities suffered from air-pollution levels exceeding safety limits by five times, 50 million lived in cities exceeding safety standards by 10 times, 43 million exceeding safety standards by 15 or more times, and 22 million exceeding 50 or more times above standard.[63]

In addition to free speech, democratization was the second key dimension of the new political liberalism. A creative cartoonist in *The Providence Journal* on May 23, 1988, included a caption, "They yell 'Democracy in Russia!' and ol' Lenin's remains start spinning about 500 rpms."[64] But for Gorbachev, the new democratization allowed the "democratized" to vote out the "democratizers." Robert Daniels described the precariousness of Gorbachev's relation to the democratizing forces he unleashed.

> Revolutions do not go on forever. Sooner or later, President Mikhail S. Gorbachev's reform revolution in the Soviet Union, as he himself has styled it, had to crest. The main uncertainty was whether he would fall back with the receding tide, or remain standing high and dry.[65]

The new Soviet political scene, improvisational and evolutionary,[66] became a showcase for volatile democratization. Zhelyu Zhelev, who participated in the Round Table in 1991, a discussion of intellectuals advocating democracy, reported:

> That opposition made it a precondition that the Round Table proceedings were to be broadcast live on television and radio. This caused stoppages which interfered with the working day. It was a school for democracy. For the first time the party was publicly called to account for

63. Murray Feshbach, "Social Change in the USSR Under Gorbachev: Population, Health, and Environmental Issue," *Five Years That Shook the World: Gorbachev's Unfinished Revolution.* Harley D. Balzer, ed. (Boulder: Westview Press, 1991), 55.

64. Oliver Trager, ed. *Gorbachev's Glasnost: Red Star Rising: An Editorials on File Book* (New York: Facts on File, 1989), 73.

65. Robert V. Daniels, "The Limits of Gorbachev's Reform: Glasnost Revised," *The New Leader,* January 28, 1991.

66. Serge Schemann, "Yeltsin's Gain in Clout Is Dramatic, But Gorbachev Still Has the Real Power," *The New York Times,* June 16, 1991.

its crimes and this had the result of breaking all manner of taboos ad stereotypes. It also legitimized the opposition.[67]

As Marshall Goldman wrote in 1991, the marriage of *Perestroika* and *Glasnost* would sire offspring of federal chaos, confusion, and decomposition.[68] Loosing the horse's bridle of state by democratization, Gorbachev lost control of the cart as it spun toward political liberalization.[69]

An Awakened Sense of History and Its Lessons

"Nothing is more difficult than taking the lead in the introduction of a new order of things."[70] But Gorbachev's "introduction of a new order" to the Russian people occurred at a pivotal time in their history. They had learned a lesson in their recent 70 years history—succumbing to intimidation is the not the way: "the hoary clique could not see that much of the Soviet population had finally overcome its fear. Tanks on the streets were no longer enough."[71] Robert Kaiser remarked that history hovered over the entire amazing enterprise, reminding all concerned that Russia had never learned to be really free.[72] But nevertheless, Russia had learned the first step to be free—not to be afraid.

67. David Pryce-Jones, *The Strange Death of the Soviet Empire* (New York: Henry Holt, 1995), 305.

68. *What Went Wrong with Perestroika* (New York: W.W. Norton, 1991), 124.

69. *Investor's Business Daily*, for instance, compared Gorbachev's loss of control with Clinton's. American politics has experienced a "tidal shift—slow and quiet, but vast and inexorable." Editorial, *Investor's Business Daily*, October 2, 1995. "Clinton is no more to blame than was Mikhail Gorbachev for the fall of Communism. Both hoped to save the system with tinkering. Both found that wasn't enough." Editorial, *Investor's Business Daily*, October 2, 1995.

70. Machiavelli as quoted in Robert G. Kaiser, "Gorbachev: Triumph and Failure," *Foreign Affairs* 70 (Spring 1991), 174.

71. Serweryn Bialer, "The Death of Soviet Communism," *Foreign Affairs* 70 (1991/92), 181.

72. Robert G. Kaiser, "Gorbachev: Triumph and Failure," *Foreign Affairs*

MAJOR CASE IN POINT

> Under the eyes of eternity August 1991 may become for the people of Russia what 1688 is for the British, 1776 for Americans and 1789 for the French: the moment when they broke with the old habits of obedience, passivity and resignation and asserted their rights—and assumed their responsibilities—as citizens.[73]

Both Khrushchev and Brezhnev plummeted into a near-crisis state of no confidence near the end of their reigns. Gorbachev plummeted further. Yelstin's words, in hindsight, were a self-fulfilling prophecy.

> We must not be mesmerized by the steady political stability of the country. How many times can one allow the same mistakes and not take into account the lessons of history?[74]

The lesson of history was that present political stability might be a veneer concealing powerful forces of change. In sum, Gorbachev entered a putrescent system that no genius could resuscitate.

ONCE *PERESTROIKA* AND *GLASNOST* WERE IN MOTION, GORBACHEV'S PRESIDENCY NO LONGER LED BUT WAS LED

What Gorbachev Tried to Do

Rule from a Deteriorating Center

Gorbachev released two powerful forces for social organization (or re-organization), free markets and free speech. But for the Soviet society, these forces were centrifugal, driving the factions of society apart. At the same time, however, Gorbachev attempted to

---

(Spring 1991), 172.

73. Michael Mandelbaum, "Coup de Grace: The End of the Soviet Union," *Foreign Affairs,* 183.

74. Thane Gustafson and Dawn Mann, "Gorbachev's First Year: Building Power and Authority," *Problems of Communism* (May–June 1986), 11.

THE NEXUS OF GOVERNMENTAL INTEGRITY AND THE SURVIVABILITY

rule from the political center. (Of course, he could have resorted to force, and created another Tianamen Square syndrome.) But he discovered that ruling from a center that had not congealed, but rather was disintegrating, was impossible. Gorbachev's presidency failed to sustain itself because its power base, composed of diverging constituents, divaricated.

In May 1990, Soviet historian Yuri Afanasyev called Gorbachev "a vector politician."[75] Perhaps a new proverb embodies Gorbachev's meteoric flash across the Russian sky: "let him who seeks to be a 'vector politician' take heed lest he become vectored himself." Ironically, Bill Javetski of *Business Week* wrote that "the ideal leader for the Soviet Union is probably a composite of Gorbachev and Yeltsin, a person with Gorbachev's power base and Yeltsin's popular appeal."[76] Javetski apparently did not see Gorbachev's power base eroding. Constituents moved apart too far too fast for Gorbachev to have a base upon which to stand. Gorbachev was left with no other option than to "sight-navigate between an impossible return to Stalinism and the dangerous currents of National Bolshevism."[77] Erupted on the political scene as a promising liberal reformer, after six years in office, he imploded as a helpless reactionary. He discovered that he had released a genie from a bottle too small for the genie to return.[78] At first, the world thought he could control events. In the end, the world wondered what events controlled him.

75. Robert G. Kaiser, *Gorbachev: Triumph and Failure*, p. 167.

76. Bill Javetski, "How Bush Could Help Moscow's Odd Couple Get Along," *Business Week*, July 1, 1991.

77. Alan Besancon, "Nationalism and Bolshevism in the USSR," in John H. Dunlop, *The New Russian Nationalism* (New York: Praeger Publishers, 1985), 33.

78. Robert G. Kaiser, "Gorbachev: Triumph and Failure," 160.

MAJOR CASE IN POINT

Insight from the Reaction to Gorbachev: What the Putsch Tried to Undo

The reasons for the fall of the USSR, according to Gorbachev's book *Perestroika*, are complex and numerous, but he apparently believed the downfall of the USSR was inevitable.[79] Gorbachev admits in his memoirs that the coup did not come unexpectedly, like "a bolt of out the blue"[80] for as Alexis de Tocqueville reminds us, "the most perilous moment for a bad government is when it seeks to mend its ways."[81] At first, Gorbachev struggled against encrusted stubborn officeholders determined above all to stay in power; toward the end of his public career, staying in power became not only his top priority but perhaps his only priority. Goldman thinks that "once having stumbled, Gorbachev found it virtually impossible to regain his balance."[82] Using the tottering leader's imbalance as an apparent advantage, the putsch plotters themselves became milestones of irony; they attempted to heal a dying beast but instead shot it in the head, their *coup d'etat* transmogrifying into a *coup de grace*. They hung themselves on the gallows they erected for their intended victims. Change caused the coup, but the coup advanced change. Endeavoring to pull the plug on change, the junta was drowned by it.[83] Change, however, swept Gorbachev out of the political mainstream.

---

79. Editorial, *St. Louis Post-Dispatch, Inc.*, September 7, 1993.

80. Mikhail Gorbachev, *The August Coup* (New York: Harper-Collins, 1991), 11.

81. Alexis de Tocqueville, quoted by Serweryn Bialer, "The Death of Soviet Communism," *Foreign Affairs*, 70.

82. Marshall I. Goldman, *What Went Wrong with Perestroika* (New York: W.W. Norton, 1991), 125.

83. Susan Page, "Crisis in the USSR.: Gorbachev May Be Finished, Political Analysts Say, But Role Seen in Curbing Yeltsin," *The Atlanta Journal and Constitution*, August 29, 1991

AN ANALYSIS OF THE HAPLESS INITIATOR OF THE REVOLUTION: WHO WAS GORBACHEV POLITICALLY?

Was He a Communist?

Although outsiders to the Party saw him as a transitional figure, Gorbachev saw himself as a member of a Party in transition. Gorbachev's self-perception was not of a Communist moving toward capitalism but a Communist whose Communism was changing. Gorbachev could not bring himself to cleanly admit, "The Revolution was a mistake." But indeed, Gorbachev tread on a fine line, too fine to content either side of the equation. "It is high time we put an end to the absurd idolization of Lenin," so the reformist speaks. But he adds, "but we condemn wholeheartedly the desecration of his memory, whatever form it takes," so the Party member speaks.[84] W. E. Butler called Gorbachev a "moderate reformer" in 1987, but nevertheless a card-carrying Party member.[85] "Purified Leninist ideology" expressed as a political "democratic centralism" and as economic "market socialism" was the creed of this new breed of party member.[86] Gorbachev left office a Communist, but he certainly defined Communism differently than Lenin.

Gorbachev viewed *Perestroika* as an evolutionary development directed by the genetic code within the socialist organism, not intruding germs from outside of it.[87] Hanson agrees.

> Gorbachev must be understood neither as a 'refined Stalinist' nor a closet 'modern' who disguised himself long enough to rise to the position of leader of the Central Committee, but as a would-be innovator within the

---

84. Robert G. Kaiser, "Gorbachev: Triumph and Failure," *Foreign Affairs* (Spring 1991), 164.

85. W.E. Butler, "Law and Reform," in *The Soviet Union under Gorbachev*. Martin McCauley, ed. (New York: St. Martin's Press, 1987), 72.

86. Serweryn Bialer, "The Death of Soviet Communism," *Foreign Affairs*, 171.

87. Mikhail Gorbachev, "Perestroika: Origins, Essence, Revolutionary Character," *Perestroika*, p. 3.

MAJOR CASE IN POINT

context of the charismatically impersonal conception of time in the mold of Marx, Lenin, and Stalin.[88]

Regarding *Perestroika*, Georgi Arbatov, head of the U.S.-Canada Institute in Moscow, claimed that "some of its ideas were deeply rooted in the October revolution and in the ideas of Lenin. Like others, this revolution went a little bit astray."[89] Gorbachev's *partinost* (Russian for "partyness") at least to his political peers, was genuine, who saw him as "one of ours."[90] But when asked "what motivated Gorbachev to start *Perestroika*?" Alexander Yakovlev answered curtly, "He believed in it."[91]

Time framed the question in May 1990, "What does it mean to be a communist today, and what will it mean in years to come?" The prelude to the answer is phraseology that could pass muster at the Democratic National Convention.

> To be a communist, as I see it, means not to be afraid of what is new, to reject obedience to any dogma, to think independently, to submit one's thoughts and plans of action to the test of morality and, through political action, to help working people realize their hopes and aspirations and live up to their abilities.[92]

The crux of his answer distinguishes the militaristic Stalinist socialism from the democratic/populist orientation that characterized Gorbachev meteoric "shooting star" career.

> I believe that to be a communist today means first of all to be consistently democratic and to put universal human

---

88. Stephen E. Hanson, "Gorbachev: The Last True Leninist Believer?" in *The Crisis of Leninism and the Decline of the Left*. Daniel Chirot, ed. (Seattle: University of Washington Press, 1991), p. 40.

89. Gary Hart, *Russia Shakes the World: The Second Russian Revolution and Its Impact on the West* (New York: Cornelia & Michael Bessie Books, 1991), 31.

90. Robert G. Kaiser, "Gorbachev: Triumph and Failure," *Foreign Affairs* (Spring 1991), 162.

91. David Pryce-Jones, *The Strange Death of the Soviet Empire* (New York: Metropolitan Books, 1995), 392.

92. Kaiser, 163.

values above everything else. . . . The Stalinist model of socialism should not be confused with true socialist theory. As we dismantle the Stalinist system, we are not retreating from socialism, but are moving toward it.[93]

To be sure, Gorbachev loosened the leash of hard-core Leninist ideology, but his unwillingness to break the leash diminished his capacity to manage the new forces of change.[94] Official propaganda, inculcated since kindergarten, may have been a yoke too inbred to cast off, even for the free-thinking, flexible new leader.[95] Gorbachev's inability to renounce his roots in the Party limited his freedom of action and, eventually, his capacity to manage the forces that his revolution unleashed. "Because he was a good Party man he succeeded; because he was a good Party man he failed. That may prove to be the ultimate paradox of Gorbachev."[96]

Was He Religious?

Was Gorbachev a man of faith, and if so, what faith? Robert Kaiser quotes a member of the Congress of People's Deputies who suggested that Sakharov and Gorbachev shared a sublime religiosity, not so much in a personal deity, but that "history and life have a purpose." Gorbachev would probably shudder at the religiosity of Bismark's driving vision of tugging the coat tails of God as He marches through history,[97] but Kaiser correctly discerns "serious moral concerns, that he was interested in spiritual values and that he felt he was serving a larger purpose than most politicians."[98] Gorbachev's valley of decision on quelling Vilnius by force belies a depth of morality: would he order the elite troops to shoot their own apostates? But Gorbachev's morality sidestepped civil war,

---

93. Kaiser, 163.
94. Kaiser, 160.
95. Kaiser, 162.
96. Kaiser, 161.
97. Kaiser, 165.
98. Kaiser, 165.

MAJOR CASE IN POINT

opting for compromise. (The reason Gorbachev took the military option with the Azrbaijani Popular Front was that his own Communist Party leadership in the area was no longer capable of exerting any authority.[99]) But at the point of realization that "market socialism" was unattainable, the beleaguered Gorbachev, left with two options, capitulated to a free-market economy over morally repulsive "at-the-point-of-a-gun socialism." Conversely, Stalin provides a dark foil to the man who apparently agonized to be humane, develop toleration, and restrain the use of force.

Gorbachev, however moral in his restraint in the use of force, does not adhere to the theistic ethic of his countryman Vladislav Krasnav, who wrote regarding the non-theistic bent of scientific dialectical materialism:

> [The old belief was that] the progress of mankind could be achieved only through class struggle and violent world revolution. If only mankind could follow through on that 'law,' it would soon be rid of exploitation, poverty, hard toil, injustice, wars, and national strife. This was certainly a rationalist, though hardly a rational, idea. It also was an atheist idea. Not only was it atheist in the sense of denying God's existence but it was an actively theomachic, God-fighting idea. It stipulated not only the overthrow of God (or gods and religion in general), but also the enthronement of man, with his 'omnipotent science' as the new ruler of the universe.[100]

Peter Jennings, several days after the coup, asked Gorbachev regarding his personal religious beliefs; Gorbachev averred to be an atheist.[101] Although an atheist, Gorbachev believed in the human spirit, and the necessity of its rebirth, stating, "spiritual rebirth is as essential to society as oxygen."[102]

---

99. Quentin Peel, "Gorbachev Gambles to Thwart Soviet Backlash," *Financial Times*, January 22, 1990.

100. Vladislav Krasnav, *Russia Beyond Communism: A Chronicle of National Rebirth* (Boulder: Westview Press, 1991), 272.

101. John B. Dunlop, *The Rise and the Fall of the Soviet Empire* (Princeton: Princeton University Press, 1993), 54.

102. July 1990, Speech to the Party Congress. Robert G. Kaiser, "Gorbachev:

THE NEXUS OF GOVERNMENTAL INTEGRITY AND THE SURVIVABILITY

Was He a Democrat?

"Democracy is as essential to society as air," said Gorbachev in January 1987.[103] Gorbachev's rise and fall proves that democratic socialism's life during the evolution of socialism is a brief one and will eventually be abandoned by the people.[104] Gorbachev himself is not a flat, static figure; rather, he underwent his own metamorphosis. Gorbachev appeared caught in a tug of war between his visionary air and the cruel realities of power politics. On the one hand, he gravitated toward the envisioned moralistic, flexible, and human socialism that functioned through populist democracy; on the other, he was pulled into the stark reality of power maintenance: use it or lose it.[105]

Gorbachev, through his remarkable vicissitudes, became a believer in the Lockean axiom that the government must not rule without the consent of the governed: "I have in mind the Party which ruled in the name of the people without obtaining the authority to do so from the people themselves."[106] As Gorbachev remarked in retrospect in 1993, reflecting on the need of respect for and consent from constituents:

> People like having a president like Yeltsin, who is good at ramming. But the method is only fit to demolish walls. To transform society, one ought to act bit by bit. Otherwise it is like Stalin: driving people like cattle, from one pasture to another.[107]

Triumph and Failure," *Foreign Affairs* (Spring 1991), 165. Yeltsin stated the Soviet leaders knew of U.S. prisoners of war in Soviet prison camps. David Ljunggren, "Russia-U.S. Team Starts Hunt for Korean War POW," The Reuter Library Report, June 18, 1992.

103. Kaiser, 165.

104. Arnold R. Isaacs, "Learning to Deal with Amerikanski," *The Washington Post*, August 1, 1993.

105. *Cf.* Kaiser, 164.

106. Mikhail Gorbachev, *The August Coup* (New York: Harper-Collins, 1991), p. 11.

107. Mikhail Gorbachev, Personalities, *Moscow News*, January 1, 1993

MAJOR CASE IN POINT

In a similar vein of concern, after Prime Minister Yegor Gaidar resigned, Gorbachev remarked, "He had to be stopped." In Gorbachev's estimation, Gaidar and his team precipitated their fall with "their cynical attitude to people."[108] Gorbachev had matured, however, politically, morally, perhaps even spiritually, away from slaughtering people like Stalin, driving them like Khrushchev and Brezhnev, or derogating them like Gaidar.

Was He Incompetent?

Gorbachev and his associates believed that the "organism could be cured, the bad cells cut out, and a renewed and healthy Soviet Union could again demonstrate socialism's true potential."[109] Gorbachev believed this even after the coup. Abel Aganbenyan, who first convinced Gorbachev of the severity of the economic crisis, believed *Perestroika* could bring per capita Soviet income up to U.S. levels by the year 2000.[110] He had high expectations; by 1990 Soviet machine-building industry would have 90 percent of its product up to the standards of the advanced capitalist societies, and personal computer use would be as widespread in Russia as in Western Europe.[111] Gorbachev and his politico-physicians put the system on the table, believing that major surgery could mundify it; but their patient bled to death on the operating table. He set to bowdlerize the system, but the system was terminal, and he did not know it. Should Gorbachev have known it? Yeltsin did. The republics did. As Aleksandr Yakovlev, his former associate, remarked even after the coup: "He still doesn't understand the situation into which the country has moved." In sum, he promised to raise "the economic well-being of the Soviet peoples to a qualitatively new level."[112] A tall order to fill for a people whose per capita real stan-

108. Gorbachev, *Moscow News*
109. Serweryn Bialer, "The Death of Soviet Communism," *Foreign Affairs*, 171.
110. Bialer, 172.
111. Bialer, 171.
112. *Economicheskaia gazeta*, Feb. 19, 1988, 10–11; Marshall I. Goldman,

dard of living actually fell one percent per year.[113] His view was optimistic at best, unrealistic at the time, but naive in retrospect.

Marshall I. Goldman, of the Russian Research Center at Harvard University, views Gorbachev's faulty decisions as a major cause of the gargantuan economic plummet. Matlock faults Gorbachev with choosing mediocre associates and fatal gullibility about the KGB.[114] John Dunlop sees Gorbachev as "out of touch": "His attempt to rescue the 'Union' at a time when power had almost completely devolved to the republics showed that he was out of touch with political reality..."[115] *The Washington Times* saw the last-ditch effort to reassert power not as naiveté but as vanity.

> Why did Mr. Gorbachev not leave quietly when it became obvious to just about the whole of the rest of the world this fall that it was all over? Why did he not simply declare victory for his own policies of *Glasnost* and *Perestroika* and retire with dignity? A combination of reasons suggests itself: The politician's vanity and love of power no doubt are part of it.[116]

But, alas, Soviet leaders traditionally left office in a casket.[117]

Soviets, seeing him undeserving of adulation, often express amazement and dismay at the popularity of Gorbachev in the

---

"Gorbachev the Economist," *Foreign Affairs* 69 (1990), 29.

113. *Sotsialisticheskaia industria*, Oct. 30, 1988, 2; Marshall I. Goldman, "Gorbachev the Economist," *Foreign Affairs*, 29.

114. *Kirkus Reviews*, The Kirkus Service, Inc., September 1, 1995; Jack F. Matlock, *Autopsy on an Empire: Observing the Collapse of the Soviet Union* (Random, 1995) (writing after having the left Moscow one week before the attempted coup, having served as U.S. ambassador to the USSR from 1987 to 1991).

115. John H. Dunlop, *The Rise of Russia and the Fall of the Soviet Empire* (Princeton: Princeton University Press, 1993), 275. "Commentary: In the Final Act of the Drama, Gorbachev Gets the Hook," *The Washington Times*, December 22, 1991.

116. Commentary, *The Washington Times*.

117. Commentary, *The Washington Times*.

West.[118] Some Soviets disdained both the message, however enlightened, and the man who bore it.

> [T]he main reason for Gorbachev's fall, in my view, lies not in his ideology but in his character.... Gorbachev always moved forward while facing backwards, so to speak, always keeping an eye on both his comrades-in-arms and his adversaries. He was afraid of taking risks. But politics, especially during periods of major change, demands bold and sometimes even adventurist steps from reformers.[119]

But it appears the brunt of Gorbachev's criticism derives from the Soviet Union's economic failure. Gorbachev's lack of prowess as an economist was an Achilles heel.

CONCLUDING REMARKS: COMPARING WHAT GORBACHEV TRIED TO DO AND WHAT HAPPENED

What Was Gorbachev's Vision for the New Nation?

Some Gorbachev analysts believe he had no functional blueprint, only a mirage comprised of platitudes. Robert Kaiser, for instance, believes Gorbachev proceeded with no blueprint, only guiding principles.[120] "He didn't have a plan but he did have a direction," remarked Soviet pundit Evgeny Velikhov. "He started by climbing a mountain whose summit is not even visible," so concluded Yeltsin.[121]

But Seweryn Bialer disagrees.

> He had a vision and kept to that vision to the end. He had a strategy, and he kept to that strategy to the end as

---

118. Commentary, *The Washington Times*.

119. Fyodor Burlatsky, "Gorbachev: Notes on a Departing Era," *Megapolis-Express, The Current Digest of The Post-Soviet Press*, February 5, 1992.

120. Robert G. Kaiser, "Gorbachev: Triumph and Failure," *Foreign Affairs* (Spring 1991), 166.

121. Kaiser, p. 161.

well. He improvised within his strategic plan as the situation changed and he faced resistance. But he failed not because he lacked a goal or strategy, but because he stuck too closely to them. His immutable goal and rigid political plan became increasingly unrealistic and dangerous to his own power.[122]

Even until 1987, Gorbachev, by his energy, rhetoric, and stature abroad, was able to forge a coalition for reform, albeit precarious, by carrots on many sticks: to the military, modernization, to the work force, better industrial management, and to the intelligentsia, *Glasnost*.[123] But the carrots were inaccessible to all the horses; the wish-lists were dream lists, and the horses bucked. Gorbachev sought to draw diverging agendas to an axis, but his focal point could not be ascertained by astigmatic factions. There are two Gorbachevs: the *apparatchik* who behaves like a status quo conformist and the reformer who wants to change Communist doctrine but maintain its icons. Oscillating between the two roles, the Soviet complex found a man who was not Communist enough for the Communist but not non-Communist enough for others. Divergent factions marched on the same road under Brezhnev but found Gorbachev to be a fork to many paths. Having taken their chosen paths, they left Gorbachev at the crossroads. Gorbachev's vision, whatever it was, was not a road map that could keep the factions on parallel courses.

The Presidency's Epitaph: Deux Ex Machina

Gorbachev's presidency culminated in two epitaphs, the morbid one of August 20, 1991, now erased:

> He is very tired after these many years and he will need some time to get better. It is our hope . . . that Mikhail

---

122. Serweryn Bialer, "The Death of Soviet Communism," *Foreign Affairs*, 171.

123. Bialer, p. 173.

MAJOR CASE IN POINT

> Gorbachev, as soon as he feels better, will take up again his office.[124]

This epitaph drew applause from Colonel Muammar al-Qaddafi of Lybia, Omar Hassan al-Bashir of Sudan, Fidel Castro of Cuba, and Saddam Hussein of Iraq.[125] His presidency's present epitaph, perhaps best expressed by Leonid Ionin, is almost *deux ex machina*.

> Even an unbeliever will say today that the Lord has turned His favorable gaze on Russia. Because one cannot rationally explain how the diabolical intrigue of the putsch came to fail.[126]

Gorbachev's enigmatic presidency notwithstanding, his political legacy left a myriad of loose ends for his replacements. As George Keenan warned, "Whoever inherits Gorbachev's position is going to inherit his problems and his burdens as well."[127]

---

124. Vice-President Gennady Yanayev (after replacing Gorbachev), *The Reuter Library Report*, August 21, 1991.

125. Michael Binyon, *The Times*, August 21, 1991. The dollar rose sharply in the wake of the failed coup attempt. "DLR Opens Little Changed in U.S., Eyes on Russia," Reuters, Ltd., October 4, 1993. When Gorbachev canceled all foreign appointments because "political events in the Soviet Union" required "personal attention and participation," the Nikkei average fell 438.12 points (1.1 percent). Vincent J. Schodolski, "Gorbachev Shifts Focus to Mounting Soviet Unrest," *Chicago Tribune*, January 6, 1990.

126. Leonid Ionin, *Novoe vremya*, no. 36 (1991), 16–19; Arnold R. Isaacs, "Learning to Deal with Amerikanski," *The Washington Post*, August 1, 1993 (launching by Maryland University College the largest educational effort an American university has ever undertaken in Russia).

127. George F. Kennan, "Downsizing the Military Presence," *Chicago Tribune*, September 17, 1989.

FOCUS ON MCNAMARA AND VIETNAM

*Integrity, Credibility, and Legitimacy
in Downward Demise*

Robert McNamara's tenure as Secretary of Defense during the dogged Vietnam years illumines an implosion of governmental credibility. Seminal insights into McNamara's role in the compromise of governmental integrity are his own *In Retrospect: The Tragedy and Lessons of Vietnam*[1] and Deborah Shapley's *Promise and Power: The Life and Times of Robert McNamara*.[2]

Underlying both these books is a veiled rubric of argument and rebuttal regarding McNamara's role as Secretary of Defense during the difficult Vietnam years. Shapley's seminal expose revolves around the ethical question of "why did McNamara urge continue to fight when he concluded the war was unwinnable?" McNamara's memoirs revolve around the difficult tension between the implementation of the Cold War Kennan doctrine of containment and the ever-increasing realization of the limitations of American military power. Further, McNamara's memoirs exude his inner tension between executing President Johnson's orders on the one hand and his own analysis of the Vietnam complex on the other.

   1. Robert S. McNamara, *In Retrospect: The Tragedy and Lessons of Vietnam* (1995).

   2. Deborah Shapley, *Promise and Power: The Life and Times of Robert McNamara* (1993).

MAJOR CASE IN POINT

In her seminal work, Shapley opines that McNamara's indecisiveness was shrouded by his untruthfulness, while McNamara rebuts that he was caught in a tug of war between conflicting realities: the politics of containment and the limits of power projection. Further, McNamara rebuts that he was not in one but two vortices, not only the vortex of a limited war but also the vortex of loyalty to his President and loyalty to his own sense of judgment.

THE MORAL QUESTION ON MCNAMARA: WAS HE MORALLY CULPABLE?

The tone of Shapley's work is conclusionary; she concludes that McNamara neither did his homework in assessing the prospects of victory nor told the truth when he should have. By means of inconsistency, innuendo, quotation, hearsay, and direct assertion, Shapley outlines a vein of alleged untruthfulness on McNamara's part. To the "man who had spewed statistics like a geyser" and the deposee who claimed he could not recall the "simplest of facts" in Westmoreland's suit against CBS, Shapley cries "foul."[3] In a stinging innuendo, Shapley charges that the award of the TFX (later the F-111 fighter-bomber) was not, as claimed, based on political and employment considerations in Texas, but a political payoff to Mayor Daley.[4] A litany of quotes substantiates Shapley's accusation: Michael Gordon in the *National Journal*, "no one is better at the selective disclosure of history than Bob McNamara"[5]; David Halberstam in *The New York Times*, "the real McNamara is someone who says one thing in public and always follows the mandate of his superiors in private"[6]; and Kenneth Adleman, the Reagan aide, "either he didn't have this private understanding [never to initiate use of nuclear weapons in a conflict] and is making it up now . . . or he had this private understanding with Kennedy and

3. *Id.* at 599; *cf. Id.* at 539 (using the term "claimed" repeatedly).

4. *Id.* at 211.

5. *Id.* at 596; Michael Gordon, *National Journal*, September 24, 1983.

6. *Id.* at 360; David Halberstam, *New York Times*, June 10, 1979 (letter to the editor).

THE NEXUS OF GOVERNMENTAL INTEGRITY AND THE SURVIVABILITY

Johnson but was telling the allies and the public something different all those years. Either way he's a liar."[7] Shapley echoes the view of some that McNamara's character was fundamentally bad, as evidenced by a "series of deceits that have defined his life and career."[8] All told, her verdict is stark; she finds him a "perpetual manipulator."[9]

Shapley cites precious little to counterbalance her verdict. After quoting Arthur M. Schlesinger Jr.'s diary describing McNamara's "inextinguishable decency,"[10] she recoils argumentatively, "but . . . why, in each of his careers, has he left from start to finish a trail of bitter enemies . . . ?"[11] White House aide John Roche some-

---

7. *Id.* at 124. On the matter of nuclear first use, Shapley bluntly asserts she never believed McNamara had "long private conversations" with Kennedy and Johnson forswearing the first use of nuclear weapons in the 1960s. Shapley at 596.

8. Shapley at xiv; On at least ten occasions, Shapley cites alleged lying by McNamara: lying about the alleged missile gap: "Warren Rogers of the New York Herald-Tribune recalls tracking the story down and deciding McNamara lied in denying his initial statement and may have lied to Kennedy on the matter as well," *Id.* at 99; lying about the first use of nuclear weapons: "many people on both side of the Atlantic assumed that McNamara must have been lying as secretary of defense—if he was opposed to any nuclear strike first use then—or was lying now," *Id.* at 124; during the naval quarantine, Admiral George W. Anderson and other Navy men were "convinced that McNamara was a 'liar' in his dealings with them," *Id.* at 177; according to David Halberstam, the "real McNamara is someone who says one thing in public and always the mandate of his superiors in private." *Id.* at 360; both conservatives and liberals joined in the charge of "liar" when McNamara admitted the true cost of the war was not between $10 million and $12 million but $20 billion. *Id.* at 375; Lloyd Shearer in Parade wrote a title "Will the Real Robert McNamara Please Stand Up?" *Id.* at 410; in Westmoreland's libel suit against CBS, he was called "liar and deceiver" for publicly saying the U.S. could "win" when privately confessing his misgivings, *Id.* at 420; on May 19, 1977, McNamara wrote in a memo that the shooting war was a "stalemate" but denied the conclusion to Newsweek, p. 424; White House aid John Roche said "before he deceived anybody he deceived himself . . .", *Id.* at 426; in the Westmoreland suit, a CBS lawyer asked him, "Aren't you a damn liar, sir?", *Id.* at 430.

9. *Id.* at 615.

10. *Id.* at xv.

11. Id.

what dilutes the stigma: "Before he deceived anybody he deceived himself, for he was a completely sincere and dedicated guy."[12]

Although McNamara rebuts or partially answers some charges, he leaves others unanswered. He repeated "I don't recall" in Westmoreland's libel suit on advice of his lawyer.[13] On nuclear first use, McNamara partially responds: his recommendation never to initiate nuclear weapons occurred in a process of redefining nuclear strategy, specifically to include "flexible response," options between "inglorious retreat and unlimited retaliation."[14] He does not deny, however, his alleged "private understanding" with Kennedy and Johnson that the U.S. would never be first to go nuclear and his public claims that the U.S. could, conceivably, initiate their use in a crisis. On the missile gap gaffe, McNamara admits he "let the President down" by telling the press that the U.S. was ahead, but he does not recount his subsequent denial—a conspicuous lacuna.[15] On why he underreported the cost of the war in 1966, he is also noisily silent.

A shallowness in Shapley's work, however, is her monochromatic answer why McNamara repeatedly urged "fight on" when he believed the war was unwinnable. Abruptly, she concludes his inconsistencies belie a positive intent to deceive. A more thorough analysis would explore other dimensions. McNamara juggled different perspectives, bombing as an incentive for a negotiated settlement,[16] obedience to his President(s), and U.S. credibility to contain Communism, for instance. And, his views evolved while in office; once plucked from Detroit to the Pentagon, his balance of hawk and dove characteristics shifted gradually, and may have even oscillated. Merely branding him a "liar" may, in a Procrustean manner, oversimplify the complexity of issues that absorbed the man.

---

12. *Id.* at 426.

13. Robert S. McNamara, *In Retrospect: The Tragedy and Lessons of Vietnam* (1995), 241.

14. *Id.* at 24–25.

15. *Id.* at 20–21.

16. Shapley, *supra*, at 431.

THE NEXUS OF GOVERNMENTAL INTEGRITY AND THE SURVIVABILITY

Further, Shapley does not distinguish tactically useful lies from the prevarication that she sees as tantamount to treason against American service persons. For instance, just days before Kennedy announced the introduction of Soviet missiles in Cuba, McNamara denied the fact to reporters—a useful tactic in light of the sensitivity of the moment. At his resignation, however, he did not say why he was resigning; in cold silence he left for the World Bank while more of his comrades went to their graves. Now, like a professor coming to teach a class whose members have already graduated,[17] McNamara belatedly confesses his silence was morally wrong.

A fair moral judgment of McNamara requires, moreover, a fundamental consideration: to whom was McNamara first accountable, the President or the American people? McNamara's and Shapley's works logically proceed from different premises. Shapley's analysis presupposes that McNamara's first loyalty should have been that of a patriot to his nation as a whole. Therefore, he should have communicated to his nation his view of the war so his nation could decide whether to prosecute it. McNamara presupposed that his first loyalty should have been that of a liegeman to his President. As a Cabinet appointee he believed he had a constituency of one—the Commander-in-chief. Therefore to McNamara, execution of his President's policies was patriotism. As McNamara rebuts:

> [To have resigned in protest of war] would have been a violation of my responsibility to the President and my oath to uphold the Constitution.[18]

Perhaps morally, in retrospect, 60,000 dead Americans and four million dead Indochinese create their own ghostly constituency.

---

17. David Halberstam, "Guests Discuss Vietnam and McNamara's Book, Part II," *Charlie Rose* (television broadcast, April 18, 1995) (transcript #1358 on file with *Nexis*).

18. McNamara, *supra*, at 314.

MAJOR CASE IN POINT

THE PERSONAL QUESTION ON MCNAMARA: WHAT MADE HIM TICK?

McNamara's Mind

McNamara's contribution to the Vietnam debacle derived from both the strength and weakness of his rational capability. McNamara's credo was, in a word, "reason": "If it is not reason that rules man, then man falls short of his potential."[19] McNamara's sociological credo was reason applied to society—"management." "Management is the gate through which social, political and economic and technological change . . . is rationally and effectively spread through society."[20] "Under-management of society was the real threat to democracy."[21]

His steely, computer-like mind, capable of spewing and disgorging statistics, dazzled viewers, but also befuddled them; why did he miscalculate the scope and cost of the war?[22] The most acute confession of McNamara, the numbers cruncher, concedes that "reports were misleading."

> Critics point to use of the body count as an example of my obsession with numbers. "This guy McNamara," they said, "he tries to quantify everything." Obviously, there are things you cannot quantify: honor and beauty, for example. But things you can count, you ought to count. Loss of life is one when you are fighting a war of attrition. We tried to use body counts as a measurement to help us figure out what we should be doing in Vietnam to win the war . . . but often the reports were misleading.[23]

But Shapley sees McNamara's reliance on "analysis" as myopia; she says he did not have a "cool head," that is, a perspective

---

19. Shapley, *supra*, at 408.

20. *Id.* at 389; 3 Robert S. McNamara, *Statements* 1009–1020 (1967).

21. *Id.* at 408.

22. John Lewis Gaddis, "From Thunderbird to Hawk to Dove," *New York Times*, January 17, 1993, § 7 (Book Review Desk), at 26.

23. McNamara, *supra*, at 238.

recognizing one's limitations.[24] His "can-do" forward look was tunnel-visioned, even sophomoric; he should have realized he could not change the world.[25] But both books dovetail to explore the enigma of a man whose instincts, intelligence, and training honed him to try to control events whose momentum ended up controlling him. His predilection for quantitative analysis, a strength, became his weakness, making him a pathetic victim of misleading audits of weapons, tons, sorties, and bodies.

McNamara's Heart

The dichotomy of McNamara's heart—its cold insensitivity yet emotional fragility—has puzzled many. "Margy [McNamara's wife] was probably the only human being who understood Bob McNamara and she's dead," said Willard Goodwin, a long-term aide.[26] Although McNamara was raised according to the belief that boys should be "trained to be free of emotion or affect,"[27] McNamara's cold, calculating veneer would unravel on some occasions, his emotions irrupting. William Brehm, a Pentagon functionary, witnessed McNamara crying uncontrollably, "as though he could never stop," when Brehm informed him that two thousand rounds of ammunition for every enemy infiltrator was requisitioned[28]; even the most constricted man can go to pieces. The emotional transition into war is not easy for anyone, but during the escalation McNamara apparently emotionally decomposed, realizing that managerial control could not check the chaotic randomness of war.[29] Unevenness of tone in McNamara's memoirs implies a remaining vestige of emotional fragmentation. In a formal, official tone, McNamara recounts matters such as the assassination of the

---

24. Shapley, *supra*, at 612–13.
25. *Id.* at 56.
26. *Id.* at xii.
27. *Id.* at 10.
28. *Id.* at 415.
29. *Id.* at 409 (President Johnson even circulating that McNamara was having a nervous breakdown).

MAJOR CASE IN POINT

Diem brothers, while in a disconcerted personal tone he blames himself for a variety of sins—failing to force the debate about the bombing into the open and open his heart to his family, for instance.[30]

These emotional expressions, however, rarely breached McNamara's aloof surface. Stanley Hoffmann, however, sees through a *pudeur* in the memoirs concealing a genuine fund of emotions, despite a cold veneer.[31] McNamara's standoffishness veiled the heart of a man, however, who felt more comfortable with numbers than souls. The tone of the Pentagon papers, for instance, was an air of "confident men—confident of place, of education and of accomplishment," speaking in the "dry, sparse language of problem solving." Rarely would moral or emotional qualms surface.[32] The initiative called Project Men, perhaps, opens a window to McNamara's view of people. Project Men consisted of 100,000 recruits who were normally substandard for enlistment, but McNamara admitted them with the promise of career training; civil rights leaders accused the program of using the poor and African Americans as cannon fodder.[33]

EXCURSUS: OMISSIONS IN BOTH WORKS

Although the two works in tandem provide a stereophonic unfolding of McNamara's public service, some lacunae could have been covered, however briefly. In Shapley's work, for instance, although the fullest treatment of McNamara available (which includes his childhood, family life, employment at Ford and the World Bank), Shapley does not discuss Kennedy's decision in October 1961 to evaporate the myth of the "missile gap" with the Soviets, the Soviet deployment of an antiballistic system around Moscow in 1967, and recent testimonials of those who negotiated the Cuban Missile

30. Stanley Karnow, "An Antiwar Protester Comes Out of the Closet," *New York Times*, April 16, 1995, § 4 (Week in Review Desk), at 1.
31. Stanley Hoffman, "After Long Silence," *Dissent*, Fall 1995, at 551.
32. Shapley, *supra*, at 489.
33. *Id.* at 386.

Crisis.[34] Further, neither work explores policy concerns common to both the Cuban missile and the Vietnam crises, what Peter Rodman calls the "Cuba connection." In the Cuban crisis, American self-imposed limits of objective—the removal of offensive weaponry rather than the ousting of Castro—constituted an American bargaining advantage.[35] In the Vietnam crisis, however, American self-imposed limits of objective produced a "no-win" scenario. Carefully calculated and limited escalation of force characterized Cuban crisis management; the limits of American force escalation in Vietnam proved self-defeating.[36] Also, no word appears on McNamara's role in the secret assurance to remove the Jupiter missiles. Did he endorse the deception of his colleagues, countrymen, successors, and allies?[37] And, regarding the Bay of Pigs, Shapley records that air support, even from Cuban exile units, was forbidden by Presidential order,[38] while McNamara merely writes that air support "had not been properly planned."[39] Did McNamara approve of the betrayal of Cuban nationals, and did it occur under Soviet threat?

CONCLUSION: THE IRONY OF THE MCNAMARA LEGACY

In the change of calculus from nuclear theory to nuclear fact in the international stage, Robert McNamara undertook the Sisyphean task of salvaging South Vietnam without risking nuclear war. The polarized and venomous debate over Vietnam comes to an ironic climax in the belated "I'm sorry" from the one, who more than any

---

34. John Lewis Gaddis, "From Thunderbird to Hawk to Dove," *New York Times*, January 17, 1993, § 7 (Book Review Desk), at 26.

35. Peter S. Rodman, "The Missiles of October: Twenty Years Later," 74 *Commentary* 39, 40 (1982).

36. Rodman, *supra*, at 40.

37. Shapley, *supra*, at 434; McG. Bundy, "Cuban Missile Crisis," in *Danger and Survival: Choices About the Bomb in the First Fifty Years* (1988), 391–462.

38. Shapley, *supra*, at 115.

39. McNamara, *supra*, at 26.

MAJOR CASE IN POINT

except Kennedy and Johnson, artificed the debacle.[40] McNamara wrote his memoirs ostensibly to counter the "cynicism and even contempt with which so many people view our political institutions," but his mea culpa may aggravate more of the same.[41] Both works, however, may fashion an unsatisfying sketch of its intractable subject; ironically, not only does Shapley appear unsure what to make of her subject, McNamara appears unsure what to make of himself in the turbulent years.

But McNamara is enigmatic in another focus; he personifies the maturation of American foreign policy from can-do interventionism to conscientious realism.[42] A cryptic irony ignites when one compares the legacy of "McNamara's War" with what McNamara called "McNamara's Law."

> It is impossible to predict with a high degree of confidence what the effects of the use of military force will be because of the risks of accident, miscalculation, misperception and inadvertence.[43]

When 50,000 antiwar protesters marching on the Pentagon watched McNamara gazing through a window, they saw a chimera of "militarism, technology, mindless computers, herbicides, napalm, white shirts, narrow ties, combed hair, corporations, obedience, lying and government run amok."[44] Today, some see the same; others an enigma; others a sad victim of fate.

---

40. B. Drummond Ayres Jr., "Belated Regrets About Vietnam Create a Consensus of Antipathy," *New York Times*, April 15, 1995, § 1, at 7.

41. Stanley Karnow, "An Antiwar Protester Comes Out of the Closet," *New York Times*, April 16, 1995, § 4 (Week in Review Desk), at 1.

42. *Cf.* Max Frankel, "McNamara's Retreat," *New York Times*, April 16, 1995, § 7, at 1.

43. James G. Blight, Joseph S. Nye, and David A. Welch, "The Cuban Missile Crisis Revisited," 66 *Foreign Affairs* (1987), 170, 186.

44. Shapley, *supra*, at 435.

THE NEXUS OF GOVERNMENTAL INTEGRITY AND THE SURVIVABILITY

Compromise of Presidential Integrity—Presidential Buck Shifting: Exculpatory Panacea or Admission of Breached Duty?

"If the President had asked me, I would very likely have told him about it."[45] Poindexter's poignant words pierce to the heart of the issue of Contragate. If the President did not know, should he have known? In maritime parlance, the old adage "the captain goes down with his ship" derives from a notion of a comprehensive standard of care; the captain is responsible for his crew and vessel, whatever he or she may know or not know. This "quasi-strict liability" standard of care for a captain implies a duty on the captain to inquire regarding the state of his crew and vessel. A chief surgeon, for instance, retains responsibility notwithstanding his or her ignorance of lethal malpractice by a nurse on the surgical team. Similarly, the Commander-in-Chief must exercise due diligence to know the state of the military complex under his command. Further, the constitutionally appointed conductor of foreign policy must exercise due diligence to know the state of the complex of operatives under him. Accordingly, the issue in Iran/Contra was not "Did the President know?" but rather "Did the President exercise his duty to inquire to the degree of a reasonable, prudent person?" For the President, ignorance of a "government within the government" should not be an invincible aegis, but an admission of culpability, perhaps even criminal culpability.

A President's buck shifting[46] to lower echelons is an admission of culpability, because conferral of constitutional authority implies a duty to police any projection of that authority. Under agency law, a principal becomes responsible for the unauthorized act of an agent at the point the principal learns of the act. If the principal reasonably suspects an unauthorized act, but deliberately plays the ostrich, the principal nonetheless acquiesces, however mutedly. Assume the President had reason to ask Pointdexter, Secord, or North about the diverted funds from the

---

45. Iran-Contra Hearings/Excerpts, 1987.

46. Ironically, Jim and Tammy Baker used a theological blame-shifting defense—"the devil *made* me do it."

MAJOR CASE IN POINT

arms sales but deliberately played the "don't ask; don't tell" game. In this hypothetical, the President's silence was acquiescence; and acquiescence is ratification. Ratification of an agent's illegal act is legal culpability for the principal. A President's decision to remain willfully ignorant is *de facto* ratification.[47]

Further, under the law of *respondeat superior*, the employer is responsible for the acts of his or her employees, provided the acts are within their scope of employment. If the President/employer hires employees whom he knows to be more loyal to himself than the Constitution they swear to uphold, the President/employer is culpable for negligent hiring. Because Poindexter, Secord, and North shared the same objectives as the President in Central America, they acted within the implied scope of their employment. Only the President/employer is the constitutionally ordained buck-carrier.

As mentioned earlier, one lesson of Iran/Contra is the need for internal oversight from within the executive complex. An agency within the executive branch could be created by executive order to investigate other agencies and report to the President.

Another solution for Presidential buck-shifting is comprehensive legislation that would require the President to report to Congress periodically on the size, function, and procedures of the NSC staff along the lines suggested by the Iran-Contra committees. If the President must report about his agents, he is more likely to inquire about their operations. Under the Intelligence Oversight Act of 1980, for instance, the President must inform the Gang of Eight (minority and majority leaders of House and Senate and the chairpersons and ranking minority members of House and Senate Intelligence Oversight Committees) if an operation meets "extraordinary circumstance affecting vital interests of the United States." The Intelligence Oversight Act, however, never defines "extraordinary" or "circumstance." A casuistical treatment[48] of terms like these would clarify the legislation, disallowing room for

---

47. Herbert C. Kelman, *The Scope of Crimes of Obedience* (1988), 39.

48. Unpublished lecture notes, November 30, 1994, Cass Sunstein, Tanner Lecture Series, Harvard University.

THE NEXUS OF GOVERNMENTAL INTEGRITY AND THE SURVIVABILITY

maneuvering through interpretation. More specific legislation would narrow the loopholes of ambiguity. Further, legislation with better defined terms would put a tighter leash on those given to the use of half-truths in reporting to Congressional oversight committees.[49]

Governments can not govern without a consensus of legitimacy among the governed.[50] Legitimacy among the governed is proportioned to the credibility of those governing. The credibility of those governing is proportioned to their integrity. Any integrity-fostering device would be a welcomed breath of fresh air for concerned citizens still aghast by the blast of Iran/Contra.

---

49. Senator Craven's words in the Iran/Contra Hearings.
50. Tom Tyler, *Why People Obey the Law* (1990), 19–39.

THE LINE DIVIDING GOVERNMENTAL POWERS

A Line of Separation or Hermetic Isolation?

The framers of the United States Constitution viewed governmental means as sacred as governmental ends. In the framers' group mind, a government composed of separated powers should effect desirable governmental objectives. The line separating judicial, executive, and legislative powers is ultimately drawn by the arbitration of the judiciary.

Referents by Which the Line Divides

The line separating the three branches is drawn in reference to their inherent authority in general and their specific actions in particular.

Inherent Authority

As Madison explained, "power is of an encroaching nature." Therefore, power "ought to be effectually restrained from passing the limits assigned to it." To Madison, an "overgrown and all-grasping prerogative of an hereditary magistrate" and liberty were mutually exclusive. Montesquieu wrote that the executive, legislative, and judicial branches should not reside "in the same person or body of magistrates." The separation of powers constructs a "self-executing safeguard against the encroachment or aggrandizement of one branch at the expense of the other." Accordingly, the *Chadha* court held "the hydraulic pressure inherent within each of the separate Branches to exceed the outer limits of power, even to accomplish desirable objectives, must be resisted." Further, each branch is the people's fiduciary in its distinct sphere of authority. Fiduciaries can not arrogate to themselves duties outside their scope of authority.

Specific Actions

The "character and effect" of any specific branch action must be functionally identifiable as within the proper sphere of that branch's authority. Madison viewed a violation as the "whole power" of one branch exercised by the "whole power" of another branch. The executive may regulate but not legislate. In the execution of law, the legislature may participate but not expedite. The doctrine of separation of powers, however, does not deny power "sharing" in a specific action. Additionally, Montesquieu did not hermetically seal one branch from the other. The divisions may have partial agency in or control over the acts of each other.

Examples of the Line's Severance

The *Chada* case provides a concrete example of the legislature's unlawful penetration of the executive sphere of authority. Section 244(c)(2) of the Immigration and Nationality Act, 66 Stat. 216, as amended, 8 U. S. C. § 1254(c)(2) authorized the House to overrule an executive decision to deport an alien. Section 244(c)(2) was tantamount to a legislative veto of an executive decision rather than legislative participation in an executive decision. To the Burger court, § 244(c)(2) was executive in "character and effect." Congress' argument was syllogistic: "we may delegate a portion of our authority to administrative agencies." "The agency has derived authority from us." "Accordingly, we conclude that we may control the agency." To the Burger court, however, the premises were sound but the conclusion did not follow.

With a similar argument, Congress argued that the Comptroller General under the "Gramm-Rudman-Hollings Act" is an employee of Congress and "if he does not do his work properly, we, as practically his employers, ought to be able to discharge him from his office." Both legislative and executive branches agreed to the Comptroller General's role. Despite legislative and executive agreement on the line separating their roles, the court in Bowsher viewed a prohibition upon the President to remove the Comptroller or to "modify or recalculate any of the estimates, determinations, specifications, bases, amounts, or percentages" of the Comptroller as Congressional aggrandizement. Although both the President and Congress viewed the membrane separating them intact, the Bowsher court nevertheless viewed the membrane ruptured by a Congressional arrogation. A principal may not confer to its agent authority the principal does not possess. Any agent, therefore, of Congress can not have executive powers. Power to remove is power to control; power to control is executive. Five years later in Wash. Airports, Stevens, writing for the majority, echoed the ratio of Chadha and Bowsher. The Transfer Act encroached upon executive power by creating a Board of Review under the exclusive control of Congress.

Examples Where the Line Is Not Yet Clearly Drawn

The line separating the powers can constitutionally evolve. Three currently controversial issues are scenarios for constitutional evolution—the line-item veto, the War Powers Resolution, and the national referendum. The federal line-item veto may evolve from theory to practice in a variety of ways. The Mattingly bill would have established the federal line-item on a two-year trial basis; a similar bill may fall on more fertile Congressional and Presidential soil in the present Democrat climate. The ever-increasing fear of national bankruptcy may fructify into a practical means of limiting wasteful overspending and outright pork. An alternative avenue of development is a constitutional amendment along the lines of the Dixon amendment. Also, the War Powers Resolution remains constitutionally unsettled. Better, however, is for the judiciary to draw the line between Congress and the Commander-in-chief before a national crisis than during one. Finally, referenda have proved effective though potentially volatile in California and several foreign countries.

In conclusion, the Supreme Court, strategically positioned in our federalist system's power play, objectifies the delineations of power between the President and "the most dangerous branch" in the opinion of our founders, the Congress. Reflection may yield a sigh that echoes the statement of early constitutional analysts—"Thank God for the Supreme Court."

An Example of Civil Disobedience against a Governmental Body with Dubious Credibility

Law is effective to the degree law controls. Political analyst Robert Alan Dahl, in his seminal *The Preface to Democratic Theory*, argues that law is not what holds nations together; rather, cultural values and prevailing social conditions sustain an undergirding belief in the legitimacy of law. In the same vein, theologian John Courtney Murray argues that moral and religious consensus must come before a legal order.[1] A sense of legitimacy derives from consensus. The ideal of the legitimacy of the Constitution, for instance, keeps the U.S. military in order. Walls and a door may regulate behavior only if people consent to the walls and door; they could tear them down. When conflicts occur between different kinds of law—"customary" in the international sense, moral, local, state, and the "supreme law of the land," for instance—the higher law should trump the lower.

---

1. C.E. Curran and R.A. McCormick, S.J. eds., *Readings in Moral Theology*, Vol. 7 (New York: Paulist Press), Part III, John Courtney Murray, S.J., "The Doctrine Lives: The Eternal Return of Natural Law," 184–220; *cf.* Tom Tyler, *Why People Obey the Law* (1990), 19–39.

THE LINE DIVIDING GOVERNMENTAL POWERS

In the Supreme Court case *Walker v. City of Birmingham*, eight African-American ministers, among them the Rev. Dr. Martin Luther King Jr., committed civil disobedience against a court order that prohibited them from marching. They presupposed that both moral law and constitutional law trumped a Birmingham city ordinance and a state court order enforcing the prohibition. Civil disobedience, to them, was justified as obedience to higher law. Under the particular circumstances of their case, the eight African-American ministers were justified, both morally and legally, in their civil disobedience.

Legally, the eight African-American ministers were justified because the highest law in the land sanctioned their free expression. The *Walker* court neutralized the Supremacy Clause by demoting the federally guaranteed substantive right of free speech under a state procedural technicality.[2] The *Walker* court weighed in the balances the need for judicial order and the right of free expression and perceived the need for judicial order to be greater. Under the particular circumstances, however, the need for order was minimal because the ministers were demonstrably non-violent. (The one incident of rock throwing did not occur at the instigation or under the approval of the ministers.) Fundamental to our free society is the principle that social order must be constitutional, since unconstitutional order is tyranny. The contempt citation of the Alabama court was not indispensable to social order.

Moreover, by upholding the Alabama court's contempt citation, the Supreme Court branded its imprimatur upon the arbitrary whim of a local official. First Amendment liberties should not be modified, distorted, or disannulled by the unfettered discretion of local officials.[3] Assuming the Birmingham ordinance was constitutional, the refusal of the permit to march was discriminatory. A constitutional ordinance may be unconstitutionally applied. Unconstitutional application of a constitutional ordinance is a defacto rights violation. If, however, the Birmingham city ordinance was

2. Walker v. City of Birmingham, 388 U.S. 12 (1958).
3. *Walker*, at 325–26.

unconstitutionally overbroad and vague, the African-American protesters did not break the "supreme law of the land."[4]

Moreover, the African-American ministers were denied equal opportunity to march through the apparent lie of the local Public Safety Commissioner.[5] The apparent bigotry, prejudice, and contempt for liberty expressed by the Public Safety Commissioner's decision is the precise kind of evil our system is designed to check.[6] The Commissioner has a constitutional right to express evil through constitutional means—assemble, march, protest, write, speak, etc. Assume, hypothetically, that the Commissioner peaceably marched with the Klan on his lunch hour and no state or local law forbade his act. The Commissioner would be just as constitutionally bound to permit the ministers to march when he returned as he was constitutionally permitted to march with the Klan. In exalting law against malum prohibitum, the court debased law against malum in se. The legalism of a technicality trumped one of our most sacred freedoms.

Further, the *Walker* decision confused the hierarchy of prevailing social values which undergird the First Amendment,[7] by putting its imprimatur on a procedural technicality over the federal substantive right of free expression guaranteed by the First and Fourteenth Amendments.[8] The court cast a blind eye to related events to the contempt order: the evasiveness of the Arkansas government to enforce *Brown*, the open defiance the Arkansas government to "constitutionally oppose" *Brown*, and the general recalcitrance of the Deep South to racial equality. Imperative to a free society is the right of expression; this grandiose imperative is commonly held sacred.[9]

Morally, the eight African-American ministers were justified because their right to peaceably express themselves derives from a

 4. *Walker*, at 307.
 5. *Walker*, at 325–26.
 6. Check but not eradicate.
 7. *Walker*, at 338.
 8. *Id.* at 338.
 9. Id.

higher moral law. In submitting to the legal judgment of an Athenian court, Socrates held that "better to be a sufferer of evil than a doer of it." By submitting to "evil," however, Socrates capitulated to the expansion of evil. To be sure, Socrates opposed "evil" through communication, but had he fled Athens, he could have lived to oppose evil another day. By peaceably opposing evil, the ministers expanded "good." Unlike Socrates, these brave advocates stood upon the highest ground—the intersection of moral law and constitutional law. Because evil begets evil, the ministers were right to thrust their swords into the pregnant serpent of tyranny. Plato's counsel is ironically apropos for the eight African-American luminaries: "a man who really fights for justice must lead a private not a public life if he is to survive for a very short time." Diogenes would not have to look far in Birmingham in 1966.

Tragically, the moral and legal astigmatism of the *Walker* majority allowed the melanin content of the epidermis again to lead to the shackle and chain. Both morally and legally, the majority was myopic as to what is weightier—a de minimis technicality or the right to express oneself because of innate human dignity. If the Supreme Court, as the vanguards of liberty, can not see right from wrong or constitutionality from unconstitutionality, liberty will "survive for a very short time."

An Example of Civil Non-Compliance with a Governmental Agency with Dubious Sensitivity: Making OSHA Work by Disengaging the Adversarial Relationship

The acronym OSHA has become in some industrial circles a profanity, a synonym for unannounced interruptions, ineffective irrelevant legalism, ignorant obnoxious inspectors, and a game of cat and mouse. OSHA, however, was enacted for the most noble purpose of law, the safety of the people under its ambit. The nobility of OSHA's end often becomes buried in the technicality of the means of its enforcement. A chief cause of failure for OSHA is development of an adversarial relationship between the enforcers and those enforced. Resentment develops into resistance; resistance results in Potempkin Village outward conformity to OSHA's letter and unresponsive indifference to OSHA's goal. Opening lines of purposeful communication between management and inspectors, however, would counteract the development of unfruitful relationships between them.

The terms of communication should be less intrusive, more definite, yet more flexible. Currently, OSHA inspectors are like popes at the Vatican—everything revolves around them. When an OSHA inspector arrives on a statutory unannounced visit, management must freeze in its tracks, something management is neither desirous nor designed to do. To be sure, unannounced visits keep management honest, but the abrupt impositions could be tempered with minimal loss to the regulatory function. For instance, inspectors and management could agree that unannounced inspections would occur only in the mornings or only on Mondays, Tuesdays, and Wednesdays. This relief for managers should not translate to appreciable loss of quality. The "stop-everything-because-OSHA-is-here" syndrome is too disruptive for the intricate complex matrix of modern management.[10]

Further, communication flowing from inspectors to management could be cushioned by a more flexible corrective code. The purpose of OSHA is the establishment and maintenance of a reasonably safe working environment. Reasonable cure periods for violations would minimize a Draconian meting out of penalties without appreciably compromising safety. Further, graduated penalties for late correction would foster managerial incentive to act on their own, minimizing the "do-this-because-I-have-an-imaginary-gun-to-your-head" modality. Joint commissions of industry representatives and OSHA inspectors could revise a code to include a cure period followed by scaled penalties, beginning with mild penalties. Plebiscites could incorporate wisdom from management in the formation, maintenance, and evaluation of the code. Regular meetings of the commission to modify the code for technological and industrial changes could allow the code to

---

10. Cf. Eugene Bardach and Robert A. Kagan, *Going by the Book: The Problem of Regulatory Unreasonableness* (1982), 93–119, 316–23.

evolve with the changes. Further, management could have the right to petition in writing for code changes, including a right to a hearing by the commission. A code viewed as legitimate by those under its ambit best fosters a relationship of accountability rather than Procrustean legalism.[11] Representation and appeals foster managerial participation in the regulatory scheme rather than their bureaucratic oppression. Regulation with representation would quell an underlying Boston Tea Party attitude.

Better training of inspectors could foster their personal communication skills. Inspectors should be cross-trained by joint commissions of industry and OSHA officials. OSHA functionaries are best able to teach the standards of care; industry functionaries are best able to teach the duties of the trade. Internships in industry with cross-training by joint commissions would produce inspectors who understand the brass tacks of those they monitor.[12] The better an inspector understands those to whom he relates, the better the inspector can lead them to higher standards of care. Regulators must understand what and whom they are regulating. Shepherds quickly learn that sheep will be led but will not be driven. General leadership training such as Dale Carnegie, negotiating seminars such as those by Ronald Mnookin of Harvard Law School or Stanford's school of negotiation could polish the basic cross-training. Regulators should be viewed more as leaders than lynchers. To be viewed as leaders, they must be leaders, not irrelevant techno-Gestapo.

Finally, a regular publication for each industry by a joint editorial board composed of managers and inspectors (current or former) could list penalizations. The demerit list would foster incentive for managers to excel. Further, new procedures for safety, rather than being forgotten because they do not fit the current legalism,[13] could be published in the journal for consideration.

11. Cf. Id.

12. C.H. Vervalin, Hydrocarbon Procession, December, 1993. Gulf Publishing Company.

13. Cf. Eugene Bardach and Robert A. Kagan, *Going by the Book: The Problem of Regulatory Unreasonableness* (1982), 93–119, 316–23.

The new innovations honor list would motivate reforms, rewarding those who innovate with recognition.

As long as OSHA is viewed as an enforcer, partnering will be difficult to accomplish. The OSHA charter needs to be restructured to create win-win relationships, ones that are partnership oriented rather than adversarial.[14] More bees are caught with honey than with vinegar.

---

14. C.H. Vervalin, *Hydrocarbon Procession* (Gulf Publishing Company, December 1993); *Cf.* Marshall J. Bergre, Richard B. Stewart, E. Donald Elliott, and David Hawkins, "Providing Economic Incentives in Environmental Regulation," 8 Yale J. on Reg. 463, 495. An Administrative Conference adopted formal a recommendation suggesting ways OSHA and EPA can improve their existing communication programs.

HOW CIVIL RELIGION AND GOVERNMENTAL INTEGRITY INTERPLAY: AN ANALYSIS OF MICHAEL J. PERRY'S LOVE & POWER

The Role of Religion and Morality in American Politics

INTRODUCTION AND STATEMENT OF THESIS

Michael J. Perry's *Love and Power: The Role of Religion and Morality in American Politics* is a call to middle ground between sectarian imperialism and nondisclosure of foundational religious premises in political dialogue. Perry lays a course of moderation, avoiding the extremes of an outright exclusion of religious discourse from the political process and a divisive doctrinal triumphalism that obstructs constructive dialogue. While Perry insists that the public square must accommodate religionists—not only their moral views but also their religious baggage—he tempers his insistence with a call to religionists to maintain a pluralistic, tolerant attitude.

Accordingly, Perry's work is a response to a variety of views he finds objectionable. Perry denies Kent Greenawalt's claim in *Religious Convictions and Political Choice* that citizens should refrain from invoking religious grounds when explaining their political positions in public.[1] Perry envisions a new legal culture that does not think of religion, in Stephen Carter's words, as a "hobby, something done in privacy, something that mature, public-spirited adults do not see as a basis for politics." Perry objects to the use of the Establishment Clause as a guarantor of public secularism. Further, religion should not be the object of open hostility, as Richard John Neuhaus argues in *The Naked Public Square*.

In *We Hold These Truths*, John Courtney Murray outlines "articles of peace" that would frame common ground between divergent creeds. In a similar vein, Perry's *Love & Power* is a proposal for the "proper role, if any, of religious-moral discourse in the politics of a religiously and morally pluralistic society like the United States."[2] Perry balances high regard for religious belief with an abhorrence of violence to the fabric of pluralism.

Although Perry pioneers new ground by arguing for full disclosure of morality undergirded by religion, his work falls short of explaining how this full disclosure can become accepted practice in policy and law-making circles. In sum, the "what" of his vision is inviting, but the "how" of its implementation is unclear.

ANALYSIS

Premises

Both Perry's previous work, *Morality, Politics, and Law*, and *Love & Power* proceed from common premises, a psychology of self and a political philosophy of pluralism. Because moral and religious convictions are self-constitutive, one cannot avoid bracketing aspects of one's very self in political dialogue.[3] Perry criticizes as impossibly restrictive any political theory that requires a citizen to bracket her particular religious convictions, either to achieve impartiality, as Rawls argues, or neutrality, as Dworkin argues. To

---

1. Michael J. Perry, *Love & Power: The Role of Religion and Morality in American Politics* (New York: Oxford University Press, 1991), 5.
2. Perry, 5.
3. Perry, 4.

HOW CIVIL RELIGION AND GOVERNMENTAL INTEGRITY INTERPLAY

Perry, pluralism is a recognition that "human beings do not have all the same needs and wants," and therefore the way of life that is good for some may even be bad for others.[4] Perry defines a society as pluralistic if it is comprised of competing beliefs about the "good or fitting way for human beings," some or all, to live their lives.[5] The discussion in *Love & Power* derives from the twin axioms that human beings can not separate their core beliefs from their speech and they prosper best in the context of diversity of beliefs about the common good. Both views—the psychology of self and the philosophy of pluralism—are sound because they reflect accurate observations of human nature.

Scope

In sum, Perry argues for an expanded scope of sources of law and public policy, a scope that includes religion. Against the putative distinction between secular sources and religious ones, which some think should be eliminated altogether, or at least not be dispositive in policy matters, Perry argues against discrimination against religious views in policy fora. Seeking a widened, more ideologically diverse scope of sources of law and policy, Perry declaims against unnecessarily Procrustean views of Ackerman, Nagel, Greenawalt, and even Coleman. Perry declaims against theorists, among them Ackerman and Nagel, who privilege secular moral claims over religiously founded ones.[6] Perry sees Bruce Ackerman's theory of involvement in the political process, that only those moral views common to all should provide a base for dialogue, as Procrustean.[7] Although Ackerman opts for the term "neutrality," Nagel's view of "impartiality" is a close cousin; views outside the "the common critical rationality" are not the norm for

---

4. Perry, 6; Joesph P. Chinnici, "Review of Culture of Disbelief," *America*, November 27, 1993.

5. Perry, 6.

6. John Francis Burke, "Review of Love and Power," *Cross Currents* 43:425 (Fall 1993).

7. Perry, 10.

interaction.[8] Rawls confines contributions concerning the public good to political ideas, which Perry considers an unnecessarily restrictive source pool.[9] Greenawalt also objects to resorting to religious premises in public discourse because divisiveness, in his view, necessarily results. Perry finds Greenawalt's proscription against "public advocacy" based on particularity of religious conviction to be discriminatory.[10] Perry expands Robert A. Coleman's thesis that biblical religion should play a larger role in public ethics. To Perry, religion in general, not just biblical religion, should play a larger role.[11]

To illustrate Perry's general argument, if a daughter asked her father, "let's have salad for dinner," but the father responded, "sure, but let's also have steak and potatoes," Ackerman, Nagel, and Greenawalt would say they should only have salad, that is, the common denominator. Perry believes that the father should have steak, potatoes, and salad while the daughter has only what she finds palatable, the salad.[12]

Perry admits, however, a limitation to the scope of his matrix to exclude fundamentalist stances. As "neutral politics" privileges secular stances over religious ones, Perry's scheme of ecumenical dialogue privileges pluralistic moralities over monistic ones. Myopia is fallow ground for fruitful political discourse.[13]

Perry's argument is justifiable legally and morally. Legally, Perry's argument for an expanded scope of sources of policy to include religion is constitutionally sound because free speech rights do not evaporate at the gate of the public forum. Morally, his argument for the use of religious sources of policy is sound because the First Amendment derives from a philosophy that conscience

---

8. *Ibid.*, 14.

9. *Ibid.*, 25.

10. *Ibid.*, 20.

11. *Ibid.*, 88.

12. *Cf.* Michael J. Perry, 30 San Diego L. Rev. 703–09.

13. John Francis Burke, "Review of Love and Power," *Cross Currents* 43:426 (Fall 1993).

is sacred. Because conscience is sacred, each has the moral right to express herself.

Ideal

Perry's ideal is to relocate religiously informed political speech to center stage. Without privileging any one tradition, Perry argues for a political ecumenicism that derives from "beliefs about human good" in all relevant moral and religious traditions.[14] If ecumenical political discourse can be profitable on the international level, so can it be profitable on the domestic level.[15] The ideal is constructive, transformative dialogue that strengthens and extends the bonds of human community.[16]

Pluralism composed of a "morally pluralistic context" rather than a "morally monistic context"[17] is "a more fertile soil of deepening moral insight."[18] Deepening moral insight enlightens everyone as to what it means to be "truly, fully human."[19] Religious traditions generally prescribe "some responsibility . . . for the well-being of the Other."[20] Difficulties arise when religious beliefs as particular, mutable articulations of religious faith—the "trust in the ultimate meaningfulness of life"—obstruct rather than facilitate constructive dialogue.[21] Although Perry approves of Rawls' progression toward a "political conception of justice supported by an overlapping consensus" of moral and religious traditions,[22] Perry sees this consensus as only a future goal because of the ideological

---

14. *Ibid.*, 42; John Francis Burke, "Review of Love and Power," *Cross Currents* 43:425 (Fall 1993).

15. *Ibid.*, 41.

16. *Ibid.*, 98.

17. *Ibid.*, 6.

18. *Ibid.*, 100; John Francis Burke, "Review of Love and Power," *Cross Currents* 43:426 (Fall 1993).

19. Perry, 41.

20. Ibid.

21. *Ibid.*, 73.

22. *Ibid.*, 27.

fragmentation of the current political scene.²³ The community of moral and religious interchange that Perry envisions is a worthy goal because a fusion of theories on common good should sprout into a consensus for action.

Means

The means to achieve this ideal, according to Perry, is the interaction of theories on the common good in a fruitful dialectic. Ecumenical political dialogue functions through "listening," "responsiveness," and "existential openness and availability."²⁴ The interaction includes the introduction of religious symbols. Religious symbols function as value preferences and ethical horizons rather than specific and concrete substance for policy.²⁵ Perry sees valuable "Dale Carnegie" style wisdom in David Tracy's advice on profitable conversation.

> Conversation is a game with some hard rules: say only what you mean; say it as accurately as you can; listen to and respect what the other says, however different or other; be willing to correct or defend your opinions if challenged by the conversation partner; be willing to argue if necessary, to confront if demanded, to endure necessary conflict, to change your mind if the evidence suggests it.²⁶

Differences of opinion foster the growth process. Accordingly, Perry echoes Hans-Georg Gadamer's argument that differences between presuppositions are opportunities for fuller understanding of self and others rather than impediments to learning. A fruitful appreciation for such differences Gadamer calls a "fusion of horizons."²⁷ For public discourse, Perry outlines four rules of

23. John Francis Burke, "Review of Love and Power," *Cross Currents* 43:425 (Fall 1993).
24. *Ibid.*, 51.
25. *Ibid.*, 90.
26. *Ibid.*, 99–100.
27. *Ibid.*, 97.

order: First, fallibility: a self-critical rationality toward religious beliefs given their uncertainty or contingency. Second, pluralism: recognition that alternative oral traditions provide a constructive challenge to one's own. Third, public intelligibility: the ability to translate from one tradition into another. Fourth, public accessibility: "a manner [that is] . . . neither sectarian nor authoritarian."[28] The first rule, however, excludes a variety of faith groups because they believe their views are not uncertain or contingent.

Although Perry's discussion of means includes general wisdom to conduct fruitful dialogue, the discussion never leaves the dimension of generalities. The complex interactions of politicking appear outside his purview, even his experience. The thorns of conflict resolution, group dynamics, and negotiation are outside Perry's rosy vision.

CRITIQUE

Positively, Perry's work provides a reasonable, constructive vision for the integration of faith and politics. Perry seeks to bridge the interstices of our diverse culture by outlining a plan for fruitful dialogue that includes religion. His positive ideal is morally and legally defensible.

Negatively, Perry's work could have achieved greater clarity on a variety of subjects: First, the substitution of the word love for religion in the title receives little explanation. The title of the work could be "religion and political power." Perry apparently believes that love, however he defines it, is the common ground between the Jerusalem-based and non-Jerusalem based faith groups, and that love should be more integrally related to American political power.

Second, Perry suggests that faith is necessary for morality.[29] For instance, Perry, citing Glenn Tinder, states: "We cannot give up the Christian God—and the transcendence given other names

---

28. *Ibid.*, 106.
29. *Cf.* e.g. Perry, 39–40.

in other faiths—and go on as before. We must give up Christian morality too."[30] The necessity of faith to morals not only requires defense but also poses significant policy challenges. For example, the Supreme Court has ruled in *Stone v. Graham* (prohibiting the posting of the Ten Commandments), *Abington School District v. Schempp* (prohibiting required daily Bible reading), and *Engel v. Vitale* (forbidding recitation of a state prayer in public schools) that the teaching of morality in public schools is permitted but teaching religion is not. If teaching morality without religion is philosophically impossible, Perry does not deal with the issue of the teaching of religion in public schools.

Third, Perry is clear that secularist claims that religionists have no place at the political table are wrong but vaguely general as to what table manners should characterize the religionists at the table. To be sure, Perry advises, in general terms, along the lines of Bernard Lonergan, "be attentive, be intelligent, be responsible, be loving, and, if necessary, change," but the nitty gritty of politicking by the religious community is outside the purview of the work. For instance, Perry omits an essential feature of political clout—coalition forging between left-leaning and right-leaning religious organizations.[31] Because the consensus-dissensus dialectic is agonally complex, the general formulae Perry advances for politicking falls short of a political instruction manual for the religious community. Perry does stress, however, that dissensus as much as consensus will characterize his vision of ecumenical politics, but practitioners in the political process are no strangers to the outright rupture and antagonism integral to political discourse, as Perry seems to be. Perry's discussion of the ideal is an able argument for a national resurrection, but the preceding crucifixion of agonal debate, negotiation, and *realpolitik* is outside the purview of his work. The refreshment of such God-talk notwithstanding, the devil is in the details.

---

30. Perry, 162, quoting Glenn Tinder, "Can We Be Good Without God? The Political Meaning of Christianity," *Atlantic*, Dec. 1989, at 69, 80.

31. *Cf.* Robert F. Drinan, "Review of Love and Power," *Journal of Church and State* 35:613 (Summer 1994).

Fourth, as David M. Smolin opines, the prerequisites of "fallibalism" and "pluralism" tend to marginalize "one language" traditions such as traditional Roman Catholicism, conservative Christianity, and Orthodox Judaism. Perry excludes "sectarian" religious beliefs belonging to a sect that are not "intelligible" or "accessible" to others who do not share the beliefs.[32] For instance, to argue on the basis of the epistemological privilege of divine revelation, such as "the Bible tells me so" would be outside the ambit of "ecumenical politics." Many in Israeli Parliament, for instance, would be outside Perry's vision for a fruitful dialectic. The authoritarianism of prophetic utterances, characteristic of many faith groups, is outside Perry's ideal.[33]

Fifth, the distinction between religious faith and religious beliefs could be more clear.[34] Perry implies beliefs are "relative and provisional" while faith is a mere religious response.

CONCLUSION

Love & Power grapples with the "no small political problem" of the integration of faith and politics.[35] Perry seeks to introduce religion into American political substance. In the current post-Christian era, when the moral consensus on marriage, divorce, abortion, and euthanasia has fragmented, Perry's work is a timely primer for religionists seeking to apply their world view in the current diverse public arena.

32. Perry, 106.
33. Perry, 120.
34. *Ibid.*, 67, 73–74.
35. *Ibid.*, 5.

THE NEXUS OF GOVERNMENTAL INTEGRITY AND THE SURVIVABILITY

THE RELATION OF GOVERNMENTAL INTEGRITY AND RELIGION

As Per the Supreme Court—The Court's Problematic Act of Defining Constitutionally Protected Religion: A Precis of Past Definitions and Suggestions for Future Clarity

INTRODUCTION: THE NEED FOR RESOLUTION OF PAST AMBIGUITY

The present Court's task of Constitutionally defining religion is both imperative and problematic—imperative because of past ambiguity and problematic because of unclear original intent, the abstractness of the subject, and the tenuous Constitutional grounds to broach the issue.

The Task of Definition Is Imperative

In Supreme Court jurisprudence, the term 'religion' in the First Amendment religion clauses is dubiously defined.[36] Resolving ambiguity regarding this key term is crucial for the purposes of communication, clarity, and continuity. Common terms with different definitions hamper purposeful communication within the legal community; a Tower of Babel syndrome[37] ensues when participants in the discussion do not understand each other. Further, the principle of the rule of law presupposes that the law is clear enough for all to understand. And, the principle of *stare decisis* requires continuity, that law will advance in a reasonably straight direction rather than a jagged jumble of self-contradictory

---

36. U.S. Const. amend. I, S 1 (stating "Congress shall make no law respecting an establishment of religion, or prohibiting the free exercise thereof").

37. Robert H. Bork, "Neutral Principles and Some First Amendment Principles," L.J. 1 (1971), 47 (observing contradictory theories of the First Amendment and the morass that results from application of the contradictory theories).

holdings. Vast analyses of the religion clauses[38] reveal flip-flops and zig-zags. Despite, however, apparent arbitrariness of the Court's *ad hoc* approach[39] to Constitutional definitions of religion, the Court has preened itself on its flexibility rather than reflected in self-assessment.[40]

Not only because of the need for purposeful communication in the legal community, judicial clarity, and continuity in the law's development, the Court should resolve ambiguity because of the importance of the matter addressed. Religion is important to the American people,[41] and further, heartfelt religious convictions,[42] when threatened, are potentially explosive.[43] Historically, diver-

---

38. *See generally, The Supreme Court on Church and State* (1962 ed., Joseph Tussman); Philip B. Kurland, *Religion and the Law* (1962); Wilber G. Katz, *Religion and American Constitutions* (1964); and William H. Marnell, *The First Amendment* (1964).

39. Ashby D. Boyle II, "Fear and Trembling at the Court: Dimensions of Understanding in the Supreme Court's Religion Jurisprudence," 3 Set. Hall Const. L.J. 55 (1993).

40. David K. DeWolf, "State Action Under the Religion Clauses: Neutral in Result or Neutral in Treatment?" 24 U. Rich. L. Rev. 253, 255 (1990).

41. Zorach v. Clauson, 343 U.S. 306, 313 (1952) (observing that religion is of moment to the American people).

42. Committee for Public Educ. v. Nyquist, 413 U.S. 756, 797 (1973) (remarking that religion, particularly its relation to government, is a "deeply emotional" issue).

43. Leonard W. Levy, *The Establishment Clause: Religion and the First Amendment* (1986) (remarking on the explosive nature of the relationship between state and religion); R. Bellah, R. Madsen, W. Sullivan, A. Swidler and S. Tipton, *Habits of the Heart: Individualism and Commitment in American Life* (1987), 219 (pointing out the important role of religion motivating Americans' involvement with their communities); "Comment, Developments in Approaches to Establishment Clause Analysis: Consistency of the Future," 38 Am. U.L. Rev. (1989), 395–96 (underscoring the inevitable contact between the ubiquitous character of government and the all-pervasiveness of religious conviction); Lemon, 403 U.S. 622–23 (chronicling the evil of religious intrusion into affairs of state).

gent religious convictions have torn some societies apart.[44] Legal coherence is essential to political order.[45]

The Task of Definition Is Problematic

The task of defining the term 'religion' in the First Amendment is fraught with challenges because the original intent of the framers may not be clear[46] and the framers never anticipated application of the First Amendment to the states. Original intent may not be

---

44. Committee for Pub. Educ. & Religious Liberty v. Nyquist, 413 U.S. (1973), 756, 796 (remarking that competition among religious sects for political and religious supremacy has occasioned considerable civil strife).

45. *Cf.* Ashby D. Boyle II, "Fear and Trembling at the Court: Dimensions of Understanding in the Supreme Court's Religion Jurisprudence," 3 Set. Hall Const. L.J. 55 (1993) (explaining that social coherence is public order).

46. *Cf.* Robert M. Cover, "Foreword: Nomos and Narrative," 97 Harv. L. Rev. 4, (1983), 45 (defining legal hermeneutics as the problem of meaning in law. Cover's premise is that the objectification of the norms to which one is committed frequently, perhaps always, entails a narrative, a story of how the law, now objective, came to be, and more importantly, how it came to be one's own.); Richard E. Palmer, *Hermeneutics* (1969), 13 (explaining that hermeneutics brings the message of destiny; ερμενευειν is the laying open of something which brings a message. Such laying open becomes a laying out, explaining that which was already said through poets, who themselves, according to Socrates in Plato's dialogue, the Ion (543e), are messengers of the gods, ερμενεζ εισιν των θεον. Thus, traced back to their earliest known root words in Greek, the origins of the modern words "hermeneutics" and "hermeneutical" suggest the process of bringing to understanding.).

HOW CIVIL RELIGION AND GOVERNMENTAL INTEGRITY INTERPLAY

entirely clear[47] because records of some Congressional debates[48] are not extant. And, because the framers could not have foreseen the colossal growth of social welfare legislation or the incorporation of the First Amendment into the Fourth Amendment,[49] "we simply do not know how they would view the scope of the two Clauses"[50] that include the term 'religion.'

---

47. *Cf.* School Dist. of Abington Township v. Schempp, 374 U.S. (1963), 203, 236 (Brennan defining the Court's task to translate the majestic generalities of the Bill of Rights, conceived as part of the pattern of liberal government in the eighteenth century, into concrete restraints on officials dealing with the problems of the twentieth century); but compare *Letters and Other Writings of James Madison* (1987), 228 ; ONG, "James Madison on Constitutional Interpretation," *Benchmark*, Aug. 1987, at 17 (Madison arguing that the legitimate meaning of the Instrument must be derived from the text itself; or if a key is to be sought elsewhere, it must be, not in the opinions or intentions of the body which planned and proposed the Constitution, but in the sense attached to it by the people in their respective State Conventions, where it received all the authority which it possesses).

48. *Cf.* Letter from Thomas Jefferson to Danbury Baptist Association, quoted in Reynolds v. United States, 98 U.S. (1878), 145, 164 (Jefferson writing "I contemplate with sovereign reference that (the) act of the whole American People which declared that their legislature should make no law respecting an establishment of religion or prohibiting the free exercise thereof, thus building a wall of separation between church and state.") with Gerard V. Bradley, Church-State Relationships in America 100–101 (1987) (explaining that Jefferson requested, as President, that the Senate ratify a treaty with the Kaskaskia Indians that included federal tax funds to employ Catholic missionaries to minister to and build a church edifice for the tribe) and Chester J. Antieau et al, Freedom from Federal Establishment: Formation and Early History of the First Amendment Religion Clauses 1–2 (1964); cf. L. Levy, *The Establishment Clause: Religion and the First Amendment* (1986), xiv–xvi (remarking that Thomas Jefferson objected to a support tax for ministers in Virginia) (describing, generally, the vague drafting by the framers of the Bill of Rights and specifically, the absence of assistance within the text of the Constitution to decipher the meaning of the term 'religion').

49. Ashby D. Boyle II, "Fear and Trembling at the Court: Dimensions of Understanding in the Supreme Court's Religion Jurisprudence," 3 Set. Hall Const. L.J. (1993), 55 (observing the difficulty in defining First Amendment terms).

50. Thomas v. Review Board, 450 U.S. (1981), 707, 722 (Rehnquist J., dissenting).

Further complicating the task is the nature of this fluid, amorphous subject.[51] Any definition will prove too narrow to some while too broad to others.[52] Constitutional adjudication does not lend itself to the absolutes of the physical sciences or mathematics.[53] Moreover, with new sects springing up, any definition, once drafted, may prove obsolete.[54]

51. H. Richard Niebuhr, *The Story of Our Life, in the Meaning of Revelation* (1941), 50 (describing the amorphous nature of values, explaining that 'value' means worth for selves or quality, but the quality of the valued things is one which only selves can apprehend); *cf.* Ashby D. Boyle II, "Fear and Trembling at the Court: Dimensions of Understanding in the Supreme Court's Religion Jurisprudence," 3 Set. Hall Const. L.J. (1993), 55 (explaining that values are never neutral); *cf.* Further Michael Inwood, *A Hegel Dictionary* (1992), 283–85 (Kant explaining the difficulty of dealing with values through his use of the phrase 'transcendental dialectic,' which in the *Critique of Pure Reason* refers to the branch of epistemology that unmasks illusions. Dialectic in the Hegel/Fichte sense is meaning derived from thesis, antithesis, and synthesis. Hegel labeled the process Aughebung (sublation), which filters what is rational into the synthesis, discarding in the thesis or antithesis what is irrational in a particular value).

52. *See* Gen. Couns. Mem. 36 (Feb. 3, 1977), 993 (explaining that the First Amendment forbids the federal government to define religion. The two religion clauses do not define religion. Any government attempt to define religion violates the Establishment Clause because government is not competent to define what is and is not religion); See United States v. Ballard, 322 U.S. (1944), 78 (Jackson, J., dissenting) (stating that the court did not have jurisdiction to decide whether a religious belief was genuine); *see* L. Martz and G. Carroll, *Ministry of Greed* (1988); J. Hadden and C. Swann, *Prime Time Preachers: The Rising Power of Televangelism* (1981); W. Smith, *The Meaning and End of Religion* (1962), 51–79.

53. Titton v. Richardson, 403 U.S. (1971), 672, 679 (arguing that there are always risks in treating criteria discussed by the Court from time to time, as tests in any limiting sense of that term, because the Court is not dealing with physical sciences and mathematics).

54. Two reliable guides to religious diversity in the United States: F. Mead, *Handbook of Denominations in the United States* (6th ed. 1975); *Yearbook of American and Canadian Churches* (Jacquet, Jr. ed. 1984). For consideration of new religious movements, see Baker, "New Religious Movements: Yet Another Great Awakening?" in *The Sacred in a Secular Age* (P. Hammond ed. 1985), 36–57; Pfeffer, "The Legitimation of Marginal Religions in the United States," in *Religious Movements in Contemporary America*(I. Zaretsky & M. Leone eds. 1974), 9. See Wood, "New Religions and the First Amendment," 24 J. Church

HOW CIVIL RELIGION AND GOVERNMENTAL INTEGRITY INTERPLAY

Additionally, a venture to define religion navigates a Constitutional "Scylla and Charybdis."[55] The Court is Constitutionally incompetent[56] to define religion[57] but at the same time Constitutionally required to define religion. The Supreme Court's doctrinal underpinning to adjudicate is problematic; the Court cannot interfere with religion, but the Court must settle disputes involving religion. As the Court must adjudicate Constitutional issues of speech, assembly, and press, the Court must adjudicate some issues of religion.[58] Defining the apparently undefinable is inevitable.

SCOPE AND STATEMENT OF THESIS

Delimitations

Because of the quantity and difficulty of literature available on the issue of defining religion in the First Amendment, the following

---

& St. (1982), 455; Pfeffer, "Equal Protection for Unpopular Sects," 9 N.Y.U. Rev. L. & Soc. Change (1980).

55. Thomas v. Review Board, 450 U.S. 707, 720-21 (1981) (Rehnquist, J., dissenting) (opining that the Court correctly acknowledges that there is a tension between the Free Exercise and Establishment Clauses of the First Amendment of the U.S. Constitution. Although the relationship of the two Clauses has been the subject of much commentary, the tension is a fairly recent vintage, unknown at the time of the framing and adoption of the First Amendment.).

56. L. Tribe, *American Constitutional Law* (2d ed. 1988), 14-6 at 1179 (arguing that avoiding the task would seem to violate the principles underlying the [Free Exercise] clause); Mary Harter Mitchell, "Secularism in Public Education: The Constitutional Issues," 67 B.U.L. Rev. 603, July 1987) (arguing that for Constitutional purposes, the law reserves to itself the right to determine religion); Note "Defining Religion: Of God, the Constitution and the D.A.R.," 32 U. Chic. L. Rev. 533, 555-59) (arguing that the definition of religion is necessary to delimit the scope of the First Amendment).

57. Kedroff v. St. Nicholas, 344 U.S. 94 (1952) to Kreshik v. St. Nicholas Cathedral, 363 U.S. 190 (1960) (formulating its view that neither the judiciary nor the legislature could define religion).

58. Mansfield, Book Review, 52 Calif. L. Rev. 212, 215-16 (1964) (reviewing P. Kurland, *Religion and the Law* (1962) (arguing by analogy that as the Court cannot escape what is speech or press or assembly under the provision of the First Amendment, so it cannot escape what is religion).

delimitations restrict the scope of this study. First, the weight of this study is not adjudication on the state, federal district, or circuit court levels, statutory law, or secondary literature treating the definition of religion. Rather, the burden of this study is on Supreme Court adjudication; lower courts' adjudication, state and federal statutes, and legal commentary appear only to inform the Supreme Court rulings that define religion.

Second, exhaustive analysis and comprehensive treatment of Supreme Court cases defining religion are outside the purview of the study; rather the purpose of this study is to zero in on the milestones of Supreme Court jurisprudence.

Third, this study shall not treat anthropological, sociological,[59] psychological,[60] biblical, or general[61] definitions of religion but only the Supreme Court's definitions of religion for Constitutional purposes.

Fourth, definitions of related terms, such as "church"[62] and "establishment,"[63] are outside the scope of this study.

---

59. For anthropological and sociological literature endeavoring to define religion, see generally D. Moberg, *The Church as a Social Institution: The Sociology of American Religion* (1962); L. Schneider, *Religion, Culture and Society: A Reader in the Sociology of Religion* (1970); H. Stotts, *An Introduction to the Sociology of Religion* (1953); Dodge, "The Free Exercise of Religion: A Sociological Approach," 67 Mich. L. Rev. 679 (1965).

60. For psychological literature endeavoring to define religion, see generally C. Jung, *Psychology and Religion* (1938); H. Van de Kemp, *Psychology and Theology in Western Thought 1672-1965, An Historical and Annotated Bibliography* (1965); *Psychology and Religion* (M. Gorman ed. 1985).

61. For a sampling of non-legal literature seeking to define religion, see generally M. Eliade, *The Sacred and the Profance: The Nature of Religion* (1957); W. James, *The Varieties of Religious Experience* (1958); J. Leuba, *A Psychological Study of Religion* (1912), 339-61 (reviewing almost 50 definitions of religion).

62. *Cf. e.g.*, School Dist. of Abington TWP., v. Schempp, 1963 U.S. LEXIS 2611, 374 U.S. 203 (1963).

63. *Cf.* St. Martin Evangelical Lutheran Church v. South Dakota, 1981 U.S. LEXIS 105, 451 U.S. 772 (1981); Sharon L. Worthing, "Religion and Religious Institutions Under the First Amendment," 7 Pepp. L. Rev. 313 (1980).

HOW CIVIL RELIGION AND GOVERNMENTAL INTEGRITY INTERPLAY

Fifth, cases identifying Constitutionally protected religion by a particular practice—for instance, flag saluting,[64] peyote use,[65] animal sacrifice,[66] or burial ground observance[67]—are outside the purview of this study. Rather, this study focuses on Supreme Court case law identifying protected religion by a general definition.

Sixth, this study does not offer a model definition for future adoption, but rather points to areas of ambiguity that a future definition should clarify.

In sum, although an analysis or exhaustive treatment of the past evolution of the definition are outside the ambit of this study, a glimpse at the key architects of thought and milestone Supreme Court cases orients those endeavoring to guide the Court into the future. This study provides a precis of how the Supreme Court has grappled with the difficult task of defining religion for Constitutional purposes, in other words, "from where has the Court come regarding the issue of what is religion?" Concluding this study are remarks regarding "where should the Court go from here?" The burden of this study is a grasp at future clarity by looking back at past problems.

Statement of Thesis

Having erratically evolved through theistic and non-theistic phases in the past, the Supreme Court's definition of religion in the future should be specific enough to determine when Constitutional protections apply, flexible enough to include any *bona fide* religion, but uniform enough to be consistently fair.

---

64. Minersville Sch. Dist. v. Gobitis, 1940 U.S. LEXIS 1136, 310 U.S. 586 (1940).

65. *Cf., e.g.*, Board of Education of Kiryas Joel Village School District v. Grument, 1994 U.S. LEXIS 4830, 114 S. Ct. 2481 (1994); Church of Lukumi Babalu Aye v. Hialeah, 1993 U.S. LEXIS 4022, 508 U.S. 520 (1993).

66. *Cf. e.g.*, Employment Div. v. Smith, 1990 U.S. LEXIS 2021, 494 U.S. 872 (1990).

67. Williams v. Lyng, 1988 U.S. LEXIS 5067, 488 U.S. 956 (1988).

95

THE NEXUS OF GOVERNMENTAL INTEGRITY AND THE SURVIVABILITY

RETROSPECT: A PRÉCIS OF THE SUPREME COURT'S ACT OF DEFINING CONSTITUTIONALLY PROTECTED RELIGION

The continental divide in the history of the Court's definitions of Constitutionally protected religion is the *Seeger* case in 1965. *Seeger* protrudes in the definitional development because the Court assumed judicial privilege over the federal electorate to define religion. By judicial fiat, the *Seeger* Court redefined a Congressional statute defining religion. In another dimension, however, *Seeger* protrudes in the definitional development. By interpreting the phrase Supreme Being to mean ultimate concern, the Court adjudicated a "quantum leap" away from traditional theism toward a wider scope of Constitutionally protected religiosity.

THE PRE-SEEGER THEISTIC PHASE (1789–1964)

First Key Development in 1789:
The First Amendment's Adoption

ILLUMINATION FROM THE ALTERNATE DRAFTS OF THE FIRST AMENDMENT'S RELIGION CLAUSES

The legislative history of the religion clauses illumines the theoretical starting point of the Supreme Court's act of defining religion. According to the alternate drafts of the First Amendment's religion clauses, the final draft adopted included the broad term "religion" as a substitute for a national tax-funded religious denomination in the Establishment Clause and conscience in the Free Exercise Clause. On June 8, 1789, James Madison proposed the initial draft: "The civil rights of none shall be abridged on account of religious belief or worship, nor shall any national religion be established, nor shall the full and equal rights of conscience be in any manner, or on any pretext, infringed."[68] On July 21, 1789, a

---

68. *Letters and Other Writings of James Madison* (1987), 228; ONG, "James Madison on Constitutional Interpretation," *Benchmark*, Aug. 1987, 17.

select House Committee, composed of representatives from each state, recommended a modified version of the original proposal: "No religion shall be established by law, nor shall the equal rights of conscience be infringed."[69] The Select Committee then proposed a shorter version: "No religion shall be established by law, nor shall the equal rights of conscience be infringed."[70] The Select Committee's language ran amok in the House, however, because of concerns that the establishment provision might interfere with the states' rights to enforce religion, including state-funded denominations.[71] The House adopted the formulation of Fisher Ames of Massachusetts: "Congress shall make no law establishing religion, or to prevent the free exercise thereof, or to infringe the rights of conscience."[72] The Senate proposed: "Congress shall make no law establishing Religion, or prohibiting the free exercise thereof, nor shall the rights of conscience be infringed"[73]; with the last phrase removed, the Senate version passed.

The consensus maintained, however, that the prohibition should not preclude federal aid to support religious denominations.[74] Jefferson, for instance, although Unitarian, requested the Senate to adopt a treaty with the Kaskaskia Indians that included federal aid to finance Catholic priests to minister to them.[75] The intention of the First Amendment religion clauses was not to prevent governmental aid to religion but to assure governmental

---

69. *Letters and Other Writings of James Madison* (1987), 367.

70. *Id.* at 367.

71. Michael W. McConnell, "The Origins and Historical Understanding of Free Exercise of Religion," 103 Harv. L. Rev. (1990), 1409, 1482.

72. *Letters and Other Writings of James Madison* (1987), 228.

73. *Letters and Other Writings of James Madison* (1987), 371 ONG, "James Madison on Constitutional Interpretation," *Benchmark,* Aug. 1987, 17.

74. Daniel A. Spriro, "The Creation of a Free Marketplace of Religious Ideas: Revisiting the Establishment Clause after the Alabama Secular Humanism Decision," 39 Ala. L. Rev. (1987), 1, 6.

75. Michael W. McConnell, "The Origins and Historical Understanding of Free Exercise of Religion," 103 Harv. L. Rev. 1409, (1990), 1486–88; Gerard V. Bradley, *Church-State Relationships in America* (1987), 100–101.

neutrality toward different sects.[76] James Madison consistently voted for state incorporation of religious societies, including a land grant for a Baptist meeting house and state-sponsored religious holidays "where every minister of the gospel shall . . . perform divine service and preach a sermon . . . suited to the occasion . . . on pain of forfeiting fifty pounds for every failure, not having a reasonable excuse."[77]

Eight of the thirteen original states had established state churches at the time of the Constitution's ratification. The state representatives of Virginia, Georgia, North Carolina, South Carolina and Maryland used state funds to establish the Anglican Church (after the Revolution called the Protestant Episcopal Church) as their respective state churches.[78] New Hampshire, Massachusetts, and Connecticut established state Congregationalist churches.[79] Although New York preferred Protestantism in general, New York never established a state religion.[80] Rhode Island, Pennsylvania, Delaware, and New Jersey never established a religion.[81] The constitutions of South Carolina, New Jersey, and New Hampshire restricted political rights to Protestants.[82] Catholics were excluded from constitutional protection in every state except Pennsylvania, Delaware, Maryland, and Virginia.[83]

---

76. Annals of Congress (J. Gales ed. 1789), 434, 731.

77. Gerald V. Bradley, Church-State Relationships in America (1987), 86–87.

78. Leonard W. Levy, *The Establishment Clause: Religion and the First Amendment* (1986), 5.

79. Levy, 15–24.

80. Levy, 10.

81. Levy, 9–10.

82. Chester J. Antieau et al, *Freedom from Federal Establishment: Formation and Early History of the First Amendment Religion Clauses* (1964), 50.

83. Daniel A. Spriro, "The Creation of a Free Marketplace of Religious Ideas: Revisiting the Establishment Clause after the Alabama Secular Humanism Decision," 39 Ala. L. Rev. (1987), 1, 8.

HOW CIVIL RELIGION AND GOVERNMENTAL INTEGRITY INTERPLAY

The Apparent Exclusion of Non-Theistic Faiths

The exclusion of non-theistic faiths by both Madison and Jefferson, although clear, but may not be deliberate, but rather a symptom of circumstance. As Daniel Spiro remarks, "virtually every speaker in the House debate who supported the amendment and provided an interpretation of its meaning demonstrates a desire to allow federal aid to religion, provided the aid was neutral as to different sects."[84] Each sect, at the time, was theistic. In his Memorial and Remonstrance Against Religious Assessments of 1785, Madison stated:

> [I]n matters of Religion, no man's right is abridged by the institution of Civil Society, and that Religion is wholly exempt from its cognizance. Who does not see that the same authority which can establish Christianity, in exclusion of all other Religions, may establish with the same ease any particular sect of Christians, in exclusion of all other sects.[85]

In Madison's day, however, all other religions present in the thirteen states in any recognizable number were theistic—the various nominal Christian sects and some branches of Judaism. The legislative history of the Establishment Clause, however, includes no intention by any of the framers to mandate neutrality toward theists and non-theists. As George Freeman concludes, religion in the framers' time was distinctly theistic.[86] In sum, James Madison,

---

84. See generally Daniel A. Spriro, "The Creation of a Free Marketplace of Religious Ideas: Revisiting the Establishment Clause after the Alabama Secular Humanism Decision," 39 Ala. L. Rev. 1 (1987).

85. Id.

86. George C. Freeman III, "The Misguided for the Constitutional Definition of Religion," 71 Geo. L.J. (1983), 1519–20, 1548 (demonstrating that no common denominator(s) between all religions exists); but compare U.S. Department of Justice, Office of Legal Policy, "Religious Liberty Under the Free Exercise Clause 9" (1986) (stating there is no direct evidence to demonstrate what the Founders would have considered to constitute a religion for First Amendment purposes. Belief in a Supreme Being was, of course, prominent in their references to religion, but more important was the idea that religion embodied the fulfilling of duties that were beyond the jurisdiction of the state

THE NEXUS OF GOVERNMENTAL INTEGRITY AND THE SURVIVABILITY

representing the consensus, viewed religion as the "duty which we owe to our Creator and the Manner of discharging it."[87]

By 1872, however, the Supreme Court apparently cracked the door to a more broad scope of religion,[88] positing a universal negation: "the law knows *no* heresy, and is committed to the support of *no* dogma" [emphasis added].[89] But, in 1931, the Court defined the essence of religion as a belief in a relation to God.[90] Hughes maintained, supported by Justices Brandeis, Stone, and Holmes, the more narrow formulation, arguing:

> [T]he essence of religion is belief in a relation to God involving duties superior to those arising from any human relation. One cannot speak of religious liberty, with proper appreciation of its essential and historic significance, without assuming the existence of a belief in supreme allegiance to the Will of God.[91]

The Second Key Development in 1878–90: The Mormon Polygamy Cases

REYNOLDS V. UNITED STATES (1878)

In *Reynolds*, the Court established a belief/behavior dichotomy—Mormons could Constitutionally believe in polygamy but could not Constitutionally practice it. Harnessed on original intent,[92] *Reynolds* set a hermeneutic precedent for nearly the next century.

---

either to prescribe or to proscribe.).

87. Walz v. Tax Commn, 397 U.S. (1970), 664, 719 (Douglas, J., dissenting) (quoting "Memorial and Remonstrance Against Religious Assessments" in *The Writings of James Madison* (G. Hunt ed. 1901), 183–91.

88. Watson v. Jones, 80 U.S. (13 Wall.) (1872), 679.

89. Watson v. Jones, 80 U.S. (13 Wall.) (1872), 679, 728.

90. United States v. Macintosh, 283 U.S. (1931), 605, 633–34 (Hughes, J., dissenting).

91. Id. at 633–34.

92. Reynolds v. United States, 98 U.S. (1878), 145 (holding that criminal law against polygamy can be Constitutionally applied over religious objection);

The word religion is not defined in the Constitution. We must go elsewhere, therefore, to ascertain its meaning, and nowhere more appropriately, we think, than to the history of the times in the midst of which the provision was adopted.[93]

Reynolds attempted to reconstruct the framers' intent, holding:

[A] word should be defined as it was understood by the legislators who enacted it. As society can thwart religiously motivated human sacrifice, so the Court reasoned, so can the Court waive Constitutional protection for religious practice contrary to the common good.[94]

BEASON V. UNITED STATES (1890)

Under the same rationale articulated in *Reynolds*, the Court in *Beason* in 1890 denied the Constitutional right to vote because of membership in an organization that advocates polygamy.[95] Justice Davis argued that polygamy is contrary to natural law, offending the common sense of mankind, hence not legal religion but dangerous religion.[96] Further, the Court perceived religion as distinctly creationist.

The term religion has reference to one's views of his relations to his Creator, and to the obligations they impose of reverence for his being and character, and obedience to his will. It is often confounded with the cultus or form of

---

Malnak v. Yogi, 592 F.2d (3rd Cir. 1979), 197, 199; Womens' Services, P.C. v. Thone, 483 F.Supp, (D.C. Neb. 1979), 1022, 1032.

93. Reynolds v. United States, 98 U.S. (1878), 145, 166 ; "Comment: Defining Religion: Of God, the Constitution and the D.A.R.," 32 U.Chi. L.Rev. (1965), 533, 539.

94. Reynolds v. United States, 98 U.S., 166.

95. Davis v. Beason, 133 U.S. (1890), 333–34.

96. Ibid.

worship of a particular sect, but is distinguishable from the latter.[97]

Additionally, the Court distinguished protected religion and Constitutionally marginalized cults. Religion consists of views and obligations; cults consist of ritual and behavior.[98] Thus, to the *Beason* Court the polygamous practice in Mormonism was not Constitutional because it was not true religion, but only cultic ritual.

THE LATE CORPORATION OF THE CHURCH OF JESUS CHRIST OF LATTER-DAY SAINTS V. UNITED STATES (1890)

In the same vein as *Reynolds* and *Beason*, the *Late Corporation Court* ruled that polygamy openly violated the enlightened sentiment of mankind, notwithstanding the pretence[99] of religious conviction by which they may be advocated and practiced.[100] Hence, *the Late Corporation Court* solved the Constitutional problem by defining polygamy as Constitutionally non-religion. Forty years after *Late Corporation*, Justice Hughes would argue the flip-side of *Late Corporation*, advocating the definition of "true" religion: "the essence of religion is belief in a relation to God involving duties superior to those arising from any human relation."[101] Post-*Seeger* cases, however, would later delineate the Hughes definition as not authoritative, but only dicta.[102]

---

97. Davis v. Beason, 333, 342 (1890).

98. Id. at 342.

99. Gatgounis, G. J. (2014). *The Nexus of Governmental Integrity and the Survivability of American Constitutional Democracy.* Charleston, SC: George J. Gatgounis.

100. 136 U.S. 1 (1890).

101. United States v. Macintosh, 283 U.S. (1931), 605, 633–34 (Hughes, J., dissenting).

102. See Welsh v. United States, 393 U.S. (1970), 333, 348 (Harlan, J., concurring); United States v. Seeger, 380 U.S. (1965), 163, 175; Malnak v. Yogi, 592 F.2d (3rd Cir. 1979), 197, 201.

HOW CIVIL RELIGION AND GOVERNMENTAL INTEGRITY INTERPLAY

THE POST-SEEGER NON-THEISTIC PHASE
(Post-1965)

This era evidences a transition in focus from the object of worship, a personal deity, to the subject of worship, the individual. Rather than focusing on the content of religious dogma, the Court began focusing on the psychology of the religionist.[103]

Key Developments in 1940, 1948, and 1952 Leading to Seeger: The Conscientious Objector Cases

CONFLICT IN THE LOWER AND SUPREME COURTS BEFORE 1965

Kauten v. United States in the Second Circuit (1940)

The *Kauten* interpretation of religion demonstrates a shift in emphasis from the relation between humanity and God to the relation between humanity and the universe. Rather than considering the attributes of a religious denomination, such as its dogma, doctrines and creeds, the Second Circuit shifted its focus to the psychological function of belief in the life of the individual.[104]

Mathias Kauten, while characterizing himself an "atheist" or "at least an agnostic," refused induction because of his objection to war.[105] Interpreting the Selective Training and Service Act of 1940, which allowed exemption from military service for anyone who by reason of religious training and belief objects to war in any form,[106] Judge Augustus Hand, representing the *Kauten* court, considered defining religion impossible.

---

103. James M. Donovan, "Law, Anthropology, and the Definition of Religion," 6 Set. Hall Const. L.J. 23, W14 (1995).

104. Note "Toward a Constitutional Definition" at 1061.

105. 133 F.2d (2d Cir. 1943), 703, 705, 707 & n.2.

106. Selective Training and Service Act of 1940, Pub. L. No. 73–783, ch. 720, 54 Stat. 885 (repealed 1955).

> It is unnecessary to attempt a definition of religion; the content of the term is found in the history of the human race and is incapable of compression into a few words. Religious belief arises from a sense of the inadequacy of reason as a means of relating the individual to his fellow-men and to his universe. . . . It is a belief finding expression in a conscience which categorically requires the believer to disregard elementary self-interest and to accept martyrdom in preference to transgressing its tenets.[107]

Hand further explained that conscientious objection is

> a response of the individual to an inward mentor, call it *conscience or God*, that is for many persons at the present time the equivalent of what has always been thought a religious impulse [emphasis added].[108]

Significantly, Hand juxtaposed "conscience" with "God."

In *Kauten*, the Second Circuit fixed on two signifiers of Constitutional religion—sincerity and epistemology. Paving the way for *Ballard*, *Kauten* held that sincere belief is a belief that the person would refuse to violate, "no matter the cost."[109] Paving the way for *Seeger*, *Kauten* held that religion consists in a state of mind—*mens rea*. The state of mind, however, need not be reasonable to or generally accepted by society.[110]

United States v. Ballard in the Supreme Court (1944)

The *Ballard* Court also focused on the sincerity of a religious claimant.[111] Echoing both *Kauten* and *Barnette*, where the Court

---

107. Id. at 708. 133 F.2d (2d Cir. 1943), 703, 708.
108. Ibid.
109. United v. Kauten, 133 F.2d (2d Cir. 1943), 703, 708.
110. *Id.*
111. United States v. Ballard, 322 U.S. 78 (1944) (granting nevertheless an exemption that one can, of course, imagine an asserted claim so bizarre, so clearly non-religious in motivation, as not to be entitled to protection under the Free Exercise Clause).

HOW CIVIL RELIGION AND GOVERNMENTAL INTEGRITY INTERPLAY

held the claimants' devoutness of their belief is evidenced by their willingness to suffer persecution and punishment, rather than [go against that belief].[112] *Ballard* expanded the scope of Constitutionally protected religion, drifting even further from the *Davis* perspective that beliefs that offend the common sense of mankind are unprotected.[113] Characterizing religion as an internal sincere belief,[114] *Ballard* marked a transition of focus to a particular aspect of the psychology of the religionist—sincerity. Indeed, *Ballard* heralded the movement toward a content-free definition of religion, paving the way for *Seeger*.[115]

George v. United States in the Ninth Circuit (1952)

Mirroring the Chief Justice Hughes definition in *Macintosh*,[116] Congress defined in the Selective Service Act of 1948 religious training and belief as

> an individual's belief in a relation to Supreme Being involving duties superior to those arising from any human relation, but does not include essentially political, sociological, or philosophical views or a merely personal moral code.[117]

---

112. West Virginia State Bd. of Educ. v. Barnette, 319 U.S. (1943), 624, 643 (Black, J. concurring).

113. Steven D. Collier, "Comment, Beyond Seeger/Welsh: Redefining Religion Under the Constitution," 31 Emory L.J. (1982), 973, 979.

114. *Id.*; International Society for Krishna Consciousness Inc. v. Barber, 650 F.2d (2d Cir. 1981), 430, 441 (holding that an adherent's belief would not be sincere if she acts in a manner inconsistent with belief).

115. Helen Yomtov Herman, History and Utility of the Supreme Courts Present Definition of Religion, 26 Loy. L. Rev. (1980), 87, 92.

116. United States v. MacIntosh, 283 U.S. (1931), 605, 633-34 (Hughes, C.J., dissenting).

117. Selective Service Act of 1948, Pub. L. No. 80-759, ch. 625, section 6(j), 62 Stat. 604, 612-13 (current version at 50 U.S.C. § 456 (j) (1976).

In *George*, the plaintiff rebutted the Congressional definition, arguing the Act was "unreasonably restrictive."[118] The Ninth Circuit disagreed, however, holding that the electoral process vests the right of definition with the federal electorate, even if the definition appears "arbitrary."[119] The Ninth Circuit agreed with the definition, explaining that the Act cover[ed] the case of most persons who derive inspiration from what as been called the "Life of God in the Soul of Man."[120]

Moreover, the Ninth Circuit rebuffed *Kauten*, dismissing Judge Hand's more broad definition as obiter dictum, and any holding deriving from it as "error."[121] *George* upheld a Congressional definition, holding that it comported

> with the spirit in which Religion is understood generally, and the manner in which it has been defined by the courts. It is couched in terms of the relationship of the individual to Supreme Being.[122]

Further, the Ninth Circuit in *Berman* added to its definition of religion the dimensions of faith and creationism. The Ninth Circuit defined faith as the substance of religion where reason ends,[123] and creationism as the view of a "supreme power above and beyond the law of all creation [that] mollifies our fears and satisfies our longings."[124]

Conversely, the Second Circuit jettisoned the prerequisite of a personal deity in *Fellowship of Humanity v. County of Alameda*, rejected *Berman's* phraseology of religious worship in the "ordinary sense" and *George's* phraseology of "religion as understood generally." The *Alemeda* court held that neither designation can

---

118. 196 F.2d (9th Cir. 1952), 445, 451.

119. Ibid.

120. George, 156 F.2d (9th Cir. 1952), 445, 451.

121. Helen Yomtov Herman, "History and Utility of the Supreme Court's Present Definition of Religion," 26 Loy. L. Rev. (1980), 87, 96.

122. 156 F.2d (9th Cir. 1952), 445, 451.

123. Berman v. United States, 156 F.2d (9th Cir. 1946), 377.

124. Berman, 156 F.2d at 380.

control because "the United States Constitution . . . [cannot] foster religious worship, used in this [ordinary theistic] sense." The District of Columbia Circuit, in *Washington Ethical Society v. District of Columbia*, applied *Ballard* to protect

> the idea of devotion to *some principle*; strict fidelity or faithfulness; conscientiousness, pious affection or attachment [emphasis added].[125]

The divergent non-theistic and theistic paths forged by the Second and Ninth circuits, respectively, would collide in Supreme Court.

Resolution by the Supreme Court in *Seeger* in 1965

The duel between the Second and Ninth Circuits impelled the Supreme Court to intervene; although most courts held to the sincerity threshold of *Ballard*, courts were split regarding the theistic threshold.[126] The Supreme Court would resolve the inter-Circuit conflict initially in *Torcaso* in 1961 by circumscribing not only theistic beliefs, but also "religions grounded in different beliefs."[127]

Roy R. Torcaso's religiosity consisted of "service for the greater good of all humanity in this natural world and advocating the methods or reason, science, and democracy."[128] In *Seeger*, however, the Court would take a step further by applying the *Torcaso* non-theistic definition to overrule the competing Congressional theistic one. Moreover, *Seeger* would further entrench the *Torcaso* non-theistic definition through a more comprehensive explanation.

---

125. United States v. Ballard, 322 U.S. 1944), 78 .

126. James M. Donovan, "Law, Anthropology, and the Definition of Religion," 6 Set. Hall Const. L.J. 23, (1995), W25–26.

127. Torcaso v. Watkins, 367 U.S. (1961), 488.

128. Torcaso v. Watkins, 488, 495.

THE NEXUS OF GOVERNMENTAL INTEGRITY AND THE SURVIVABILITY

THE UNITED STATES V. SEEGER HIGHMARK (1965)

In *Seeger*, the Court oriented the Ballard sincerity test to beliefs that occupy the same place as traditional theistic religions, that is, beliefs functionally equivalent to theistic conceptions. The Court analyzed the psychology of belief structurally, meaning, they saw traditional religions placing a Supreme Being as the highest value, and held that a non-theistic analog, as the highest value, passes Constitutional muster. The Court concluded that it that should not discriminate in favor of a belief in a personal deity, which occupies specific coordinates in one's mental structure, over other beliefs which hold the same coordinates.[129] *Seeger's* thaumaturgic terms to define religion are a Constitutional highmark: "a sincere and meaningful belief occupying in the life of its possessor a place parallel to that filled by God."[130] The *Seeger* Court labeled the specific coordinate with Paul Tillich's nomenclature, the "ultimate concern."[131] Hence, *Seeger's* Tillich analysis focused on the priority, not substance, of belief.

Tillich explained the ultimate concern as "that which concerns one [which] ultimately becomes holy. The awareness of the holy is awareness of presence of the divine, namely of the content of our ultimate concern." In defining "concern," Tillich said:

> [W]e are involved in it, that a part of ourselves is in it, that we participate with our hearts. And it means even more than that. It points to the way in which we are involved, namely anxiously. . . . The wisdom of our language often identifies concern with anxiety. Wherever we are involved we feel anxiety. There are many things which interest us, which provoke our compassion or horror. But they are not our real concern; they do not

---

129. Seeger, 380 U.S. (1965), 163, 166.

130. Seeger, 163.

131. Note "Toward a Constitutional Definition" at 31; United States v. Jakobson, 325 F.2d (2nd Cir. 1963), 409, 415 (praising Professor Tillich as a theologian of high distinction and wide influence, who has taught at great universities on both sides of the Atlantic).

produce this driving, torturing anxiety which is present when we are genuinely and seriously concerned.[132]

Ultimate concern, therefore, implies the martyrdom standard of *Kauten*.[133] As the Eighth Circuit in *Wiggins v. Sargent*[134] correctly interpreted *Seeger*; a notion identified as secular does not mean it cannot become religious for Constitutional purposes.[135]

The *Seeger* Court, however, faced with the alleged unconstitutionality of section 6(j) of the Universal Military Training and Service Act, could have ruled the Supreme Being phraseology unconstitutional. The Court opted, however, to construe the phrase so broadly that it redefined the definition to encompass nontheism.[136] The *Seeger* decision was widely criticized for "distorting the plain meaning of the words in the statute and for disregarding Congress' intention to exclude nontheists from exemption."[137] In

---

132. Paul Tillich, *The Essential Tillich: An Anthology of the Writings of Paul Tillich* (1987), 33.

133. 133 F.2d (2d Cir. 1943), 703, 708 (stating that "[r]eligious belief arises from a sense of the inadequacy of reason as a means of relating the individual to this fellow men and to his universe . . . requiring the believer to disregard elementary self-interest and to accept martyrdom in preference to transgressing its tenets").

134. 753 F.2d 663 (8th Cir. 1985), 663.

135. 753 F.2d (8th Cir. 1985), 663, 666.

136. 380 U.S. (1965), 163

137. See, e.g., Jesse Choper, Defining Religion, at 595) (Choper arguing that jurists are incompetent to adjudicate Tillich's theology: "Tillich's writings occupy volumes and are directed at theologians and lay believers, not lawyers. To extract from them the phrase 'ultimate concern' and instruct judges to apply it as a legal formula seriously underestimates the subtlety of Tillich's thought and overestimates the theological sophistication of the participants in the legal process. To the doctrine that jurists' focus should be more upon the psychology of belief rather than the content of belief, Choper responds inimically to the *Seeger* analysis.) *Id.* at 599. Choper concedes, however, that Deists and Universalists would not pass muster under his own analysis, but urges that they would enjoy protection by the Free Speech clause. *Id.* at 600; *contra* Worthing however, who criticizes the ultimate concern definition of religion as anti-libertarian, that is, too narrow. Worthing at 321.

THE NEXUS OF GOVERNMENTAL INTEGRITY AND THE SURVIVABILITY

dismay, Justice Harlan called *Seeger* a "remarkable feat of judicial surgery."[138]

WELSH V. UNITED STATES (1970)

Echoing *Seeger, Welsh* focused on conscience as the determinative factor in delineating Constitutionally protected religion.[139] The Court focused on those whose "consciences, spurred by deeply held moral, theistical or religious beliefs, would give them no rest or peace if they allowed themselves to become a part or an instrument of war." In *Welsh*, the Court interpreted section 6(j) of the Military Act again, holding that a conscientious objector's opposition to war must be grounded in "strong ethics."[140] *Welsh* overturned *Berman* by completely transforming the statute by reading out of it any distinction between religiously acquired beliefs and those deriving from essentially political, sociological, or philosophical views or a merely personal moral code.[141] Equating religion with conscience, the Court transposed religion to include life-controlling morality: "what the Free Exercise clause protects is the free exercise of religion as the free exercise of conscience."[142] The pregnant phrase "a place parallel to that filled by God,"

---

138. *Cf.* Welsh v. United States, 398 U.S. (1970, 333, 351).

139. Ibid.

140. 398 U.S. (1970), 333, 339–40.

141. Herman, 26 Loy. L. Rev. 101–102.

142. The IRS, however, interprets *Welsh* as fact sensitive, specifically a conscientious objection case not relevant to tax-exemption criteria. The IRS read *Seeger* as a Constitutional case, citing it for the proposition that serious Constitutional difficulties would be presented if section 501(c)(3) were interpreted to exclude even those beliefs that do not encompass a Supreme Being in the conventional sense, such as Taoism, Buddhism, and secular humanism. Exempt Organization Handbook, IRM 7751, s 344.2) (District of Nebraska disagreeing). Womens' Services, P.C. v. Thone, 483 F.Supp., (D.C. Neb. 1979), 1022, 1035 (studiously framing the conscientious objector issue narrowly as one of statutory rather than, Constitutional, construction).

HOW CIVIL RELIGION AND GOVERNMENTAL INTEGRITY INTERPLAY

articulated in both *Seeger* and *Welsh*, marks the landmark transition away from theistic exclusivism.[143]

More Recent Key Developments

UNITED STATES V. YODER: THE AMISH SCHOOL EXEMPTION CASE (1972)

Opting for a stricter test of religiosity, the relative extremity of the Amish swayed the *Yoder* Court to allow a school exemption because of religion. The Court significantly constricted the *Seeger/Welsh* ambit, implying that getting out of school requires an extremely religious lifestyle, but beating the draft requires only a pervasive influence of conscience. Although a student adherent of Thoreau's religion could not Constitutionally pass muster to skip high school, the organizational demands and religious history of the strict Amish community swayed the Court in their favor.[144] Justice Douglas held in his dissent in *Yoder* that Thoreau's religion, which passes the *Seeger/Welsh* muster, is really no religion at all.[145] The Court to date, however, has steered clear of clarifying the bifurcated definition of religion expressed in the distinct *Yoder* and

---

143. United States v. Seeger, 380 U.S. (1965), 163; Welsh v. United States, 398 U.S. (1970), 333, 340; *contra* United States ex rel. Phillips v. Downer, 135 F.2d 521 (2d Cir. 1943) (reversing a district court's ruling that an objector's opposition to war derives from definitely traceable religious belief or training); Berman v. United States, 156 F.2d 377 (9th Cir. 1946) (denying a claimant a conscientious objector exemption where opposition to war did not derive from religious training, belief, or practice).

Steven Collier, for instance, objects the *Seeger/Welsh* analysis as judicial excess. Collier sees *Seeger/Welsh* as requiring a valuation of belief so great the adherent would endure martyrdom. Ordinary believers, not the stuff of which martyrs are made, would be unprotected. Collier at 995. To accommodate non-martyrs, Colliers suggests an organizational requirement. Collier at 995. Collier, perhaps, enters another excess. While urging protection of the casually religious, Collier dissuades from protection of unique, personal religious beliefs. Steven D. Collier, Comment, Beyond Seeger/Welsh: Redefining Religion Under the Constitution, 31 Emory L.J. 973, 979 (1982).

144. 406 U.S. 205, 247–48 (Douglas, J., dissenting in part).

145. 406 U.S. at 247–48.

Seeger analysis.¹⁴⁶ Accordingly, lower courts have attempted an amalgam of psychological/structural definition of *Seeger* and the historical/organizational definition of *Yoder*.

MALNAK V. MAHARISHI YOGI: THE THIRD CIRCUIT AMALGAM OF THE YODER AND SEEGER DEFINITIONS (1979)

Concluding that case law does not provide a single cogent definition, except that traditional theism is too narrow,¹⁴⁷ Judge Adams of the Third Circuit pioneers a unique three-part definition of religion in *Malnak*. Adams seeks to implement *Seeger* by applying three thresholds: the nature of the ideas, their comprehensiveness, and any aspects that may be functional analogs to traditional ritual and organization.¹⁴⁸ First, the nature of ideas criterion focuses upon the ultimate nature of the ideas as the most important and convincing evidence that they should be treated as religious.¹⁴⁹ Second, the comprehensiveness criterion requires that such ultimate concerns be connected with one another. Isolated beliefs which bear no demonstrable relationship fail this test.¹⁵⁰ Third, religion must have a social dimension, that is, ritual. Adams distinguishes between hard-core political activists attending a party meeting from weak believers attending a religious ceremony. A weak theist qualifies while a political zealot does not.¹⁵¹ Adams' approach, while applying *Seeger*, actually alters its burden, weighing cognitive and social dimensions more than the psychology of belief.¹⁵²

Significantly, Adams in *Malnak* assumed the courts, not the religions themselves, must decide what is religion: "the question

---

146. Roemer v. Board of Public Works of Maryland, 426 U.S. (1976), 736.
147. 592 F.2d (3d Cir. 1979), 197.
148. Id.
149. Id.
150. Id.
151. Id.
152. James M. Donovan, "Law, Anthropology, and the Definition of Religion," 6 Set. Hall Const. L.J. (1995), 23, 25–26.

HOW CIVIL RELIGION AND GOVERNMENTAL INTEGRITY INTERPLAY

of the definition for religion for [F]irst [A]mendment purposes is one for the courts, and is not controlled by the subjective perceptions of believers."[153] In *Malnak*, a system of ideas constituted a religion, even though those who claimed the ideas claimed secularity.[154] In the same vein, the Third Circuit in *Womens' Services* held that the mere labeling of something as coming within a religious area by theologians does not make that area religious for First Amendment purposes.[155] Nevertheless, both *Malnak* and *Womens' Services* establish a social requirement, that claimants to First Amendment protection be participants in organizations.[156]

AFRICA V. AMERICAN CHRISTIAN MOVEMENT FOR LIFE (MOVE): THE THIRD CIRCUIT'S FOUR-POINT DEFINITION (1981)

The *Africa* decision determined that a court must decide if a preponderance of evidence demonstrate a sincere religiosity.[157] Specifically, religiosity includes views that address fundamental and ultimate queries into imponderables, are comprehensive in nature, and are marked with some formal and external signs. External signs may include formal services, ceremonies, clergy, organization, propagation, and holidays.[158] The *Africa* criteria for Constitutional protection are:

> (1) a belief regarding the meaning of life;
>
> (2) a psychological commitment by the individual adherent (or in a group, by the members generally) to this belief;

---

153. 592 F.2d (3d Cir. 1979) (per curiam), 197, 200; Thone, 483 F.Supp. at 1032.

154. Malnak, 592 F.2d at 199.

155. Womens' Services, 483 F.Supp. at 1040.

156. Malnak v. Yogi, 592 F.2d 1976 (3d Cir. 1979) (per curiam), 199–200, as in Wisconsin v. Yoder, 406 U.S. (1972), 205, 225.

157. Africa v. Pennsylvania 662 F.2d (3d Cir. 1981), 1025.

158. Africa v. Pennsylvania 662 F.2d (3d Cir. 1981), 1025, (quoting Malnak v. Yogi, 592 F.2d (3d Cir. 1979), 197, 209.

(3) a system of moral practice resulting from adherence to this belief; and

(4) an acknowledgment by its adherent that the belief (or belief system) is their exclusive or supreme system of ultimate beliefs.[159]

---

159. Africa v. Pennsylvania 662 F.2d 1025 (3d Cir. 1981); the IRS, to alleviate the fluidity of Supreme Court jurisprudence, drafted a fourteen-point test. Bruce J. Casino, I Know It When I See It: Mail-Order Ministry Tax Fraud and the Problem of a Constitutionally Acceptable Definition of Religion, 25 Am. Crim. L. Rev. 113, 139–40 (1987) (arguing the lengthy test is subjective and highly questionable). The IRS fourteen-point test is:
(1) a distinct legal existence
(2) a recognized creed
(3) recognized form of worship
(4) a definite and distinct ecclesiastical government
(5) a formal code of doctrine and discipline
(6) a distinct religious history
(7) a membership not associated with any other church or denomination
(8) an organization of ordained ministers
(9) ordained ministers selected after completing prescribed studies
(10) a literature of its own
(11) established places of worship and regular congregations
(12) regular religious services
(13) Sunday schools for religious instruction of the young
(14) schools for the preparation of its ministers.

Jerome Jurtz, Remarks of IRS Commissioner Jerome Kurtz Before the PLI Seventh Biennial Conference on Tax Planning (Jan. 9, 1978), in Fed. Taxes (P-H) P54 (1978), , 820; Edward McGlynn Gaffey, "Governmental Definition of Religion: The Rise and Fall of the IRS Regulations on an Integrated Auxiliary of a Church," 25 Val. U. L. Rev. (1991), 203, 222 . Gaffney, for instance, holds that each criterion of the IRS test is fundamentally flawed, probably violating the First Amendment and favoring the large, formal, well-established churches. Gaffney opines that these criteria leave no room for unrestricted or loosely structured religious societies, such as the Society of Friends (Quakers) or the Christian Scientists, who undoubtedly enjoy the protection of the First Amendment Religion Clause. Id. at 209. For example, the Brazilian Candomble African spirit-possession cult fails on eight of the measures, meaning that a terreiro—the culthouse of Candomble—is not a church in sight of the government. Jim Afer, *The Taste of Blood: Spirit Possession in Brazilian Candomble* (1991); Edward McGlynn Gaffey, "Governmental Definition of Religion: The Rise and Fall of the IRS Regulations on an Integrated Auxiliary of a Church," 25 Val. U. L. Rev. (1991, 203, 222 (explaining integrated auxiliaries).

In *Africa*, the Third Circuit ruled that American Christian Movement for Life (MOVE)[160] was not a religion. The Third Circuit denied Constitutional status because of the organization's lack of a functional equivalent of the Ten Commandments.[161]

A SUMMARY OF DEFINITIONAL DEVELOPMENT: CURRENT QUALIFIERS OF CONSTITUTIONALLY PROTECTED RELIGION

Current case law qualifies constitutionally protected religion more by what it is not than what it is. Accordingly, negative qualifiers outweigh positive qualifiers.

Negative Qualifiers

A mere claim that a belief is religious does not meet Constitutional muster.[162] Courts need not defer to a claimant's characterization of their beliefs or actions as non-religious.[163] The particular religion need not be acceptable, comprehensible, or logical to others.[164] Indeed, one is Constitutionally entitled to believe what one can not prove.[165] It may even be deemed odd or erratic by the Court;[166] the definition of religion should not turn on judicial perception

---

160. "Radical Cult Bombed by Philadelphia Police Resulting Blaze Spreads to 50 or 60 Homes," Los Angeles Times, May 14, 1985, at 1; *cf.* "Comment: Defining Religion," at 550–51.

161. Africa v. Pennsylvania, 662 F.2d (3d Cir. 1981), 1025.

162. Wisconsin v. Yoder, 406 U.S. (1972), 205, 209; United States v. Seeger, 380 U.S. (1965), 163, 184.

163. Welsh v. United States, 398 U.S. (1970), 333, 341; Malnak v. Yogi, 592 F.2d (3d Cir. 1979), 197.

164. Thomas v. Review Bd. of Indiana Employment Sec. Div., 450 U.S. (1981), 707, 713 (circumscribing all beliefs based on religion as protected by the Free Exercise clause).

165. United States v. Ballard, 322 U.S. (1944), 78, 86.

166. Wisconsin v. Yoder, 406 U.S. (1972), 205, 224.

THE NEXUS OF GOVERNMENTAL INTEGRITY AND THE SURVIVABILITY

or consensus.[167] The Court in 1944 considered more broadly that intellectual freedom embraces the right to maintain theories of life and death and of the hereafter that are rank heresy to followers of orthodox faiths.[168] A religious belief need not be central to a claimant's religion,[169] in total agreement with co-religionists, be unwavering,[170] be held by a mature convert[171] or derived from an organization.[172] Religion does not have to derive from a tenet, belief, or teaching of any established sect or church[173] or involve a personal deity or deities.[174]

Positive Qualifiers

The chief positive qualifier is that a religious claimant must be sincere.[175] A belief system that is ethical may pass muster as a Constitutionally designated religion if the belief system is held with

---

167. Thomas v. Review Bd. of Indiana Employment Sec. Div., 450 U.S. (1981), 707, 713.

168. United States v. Ballard, 322 U.S. (1944), 78, 86–87.

169. Lyng v. Northwest Indian Cemetery Protective Assn, 485 U.S. (1988), 439, 451.

170. Thomas at 715–16.

171. Hobbie v. Unemployment Appeals Commn, 480 U.S. (1987), 136.

172. Frazee v. Illinois Dept of Empl. Sec. 489 U.S. (1989), 829.

173. Frazee v. Illinois Dept of Employment Sec., 489 U.S. (1989), 829, 834 (ruling that a party's religion was protected under the Free Exercise Clause even though those beliefs were not attributable to any particular sect).

174. County of Allegheny v. American Civil Liberties Union, 492 U.S. (1989), 573, 589–90, 605 n.55; Wallace v. Jaffree, 472 U.S. (1985), 38, 52–55 ; Welsh v. United States, 398 U.S. (1970), 333; United States v. Seeger, 380 U.S. (1965), 163; Torasco v. Watkins, 367 U.S. (1961), 488, 495.

175. United States v. Ballard, 322 U.S. (1944), 78 (granting nevertheless an exemption that one can, of course, imagine an asserted claim so bizarre, so clearly non-religious in motivation, as not to be entitled to protection under the Free Exercise Clause).

HOW CIVIL RELIGION AND GOVERNMENTAL INTEGRITY INTERPLAY

the strength of traditional religious convictions,[176] but the belief system must constitute the highest priority for the adherent.[177]

PROSPECT—TOWARD PARAMETERS FOR FUTURE CLARITY: THE NEED FOR CLARITY IN FORTHCOMING DEFINITIONS

Erratic doctrinal interpretations derive from an absence of consensus over a Constitutional definition of religion. Although consensus building in this vital area is difficult, consensus building is imperative for a coherent rule of law.

The Challenge of Clarity

The onus of the Supreme Court's task of defining religion focuses neither on philosophical inquiry, lexical drafting, or sociological discovery, but on policy-making.[178] Policy-making in matters of conscience is a delicate task.[179] Justice Brennan, quoting Constitutional Convention Maryland Representative Daniel Carroll, remarked that "rights of conscience are, in their nature, of peculiar delicacy, and will little bear the gentlest touch of governmental hand."[180] In agreement, the Court in *Thomas* confessed that "determination of what is a religious belief or practice is more often than not a difficult and delicate task." Indeed, every definition is politically dangerous.[181]

---

176. Frazee, 489 U.S. at 833 (holding that states can make all necessary inquiry that an ample predicate for invocation of the religion clause exists).

177. Welsh v. United States, 398 U.S. (1970), 333, 339; United States v. Seeger, 380 U.S. (1965), 163, 184–85.

178. *Cf.* Mary Harter Mitchell, "Secularism in Public Education: The Constitutional Issues," 67 B.U.L. Rev., July 1987, 603.

179. Thomas v. Review Board, 450 U.S. (1981), 707, 714.

180. Schempp, 374 U.S. 203, 231 (Brennan, J., concurring) (quoting Representative Carroll in debate regarding the proposed Bill of Rights, August 15, 1789).

181. R. Stark and C. Glock, *Patterns of Religious Commitment, American*

THE NEXUS OF GOVERNMENTAL INTEGRITY AND THE SURVIVABILITY

The Challenge Philosophically

But underlying the Constitutional dilemma is the challenge of understanding the most comprehensive yet abstract subject of the philosophical sciences—divinity. Further complicating the philosophical problem is the professional competence of attorneys, judges, and Justices to broach the subject;[182] they are trained in law, not religion. George C. Freeman III gives up on the prospect, resignedly claiming that defining religion is an exercise in futility.[183] The complexity and abstraction of religion notwithstanding, the American people call themselves a religious people, and they have chosen to be ruled by law they can understand.

The Challenge Constitutionally

A leap toward clarity by the Court, however, proceeds from tenuous ground. Conflicting concerns juxtapose the Court between horns of a policy dilemma; some argue that the Court should not touch religion with anything less than a ten-foot pole.[184] Others counter that since the Court has to deal with religion anyway, it should take the bull by the horns.[185] In the hands-off faction, Sharon L. Worthing ably illustrates the problem.

> [I]f government can define what is a church, it can also define what is not a church, and can do so in a manner which excludes religions which are not favored by government officials. The very existence of such a power would be unconstitutional under the Establishment Clause.[186]

Piety: The Nature of Religious Commitment (1968), 11.

182. P. Kauper, Religion and the Constitution (1964), 24–25.

183. George C. Freeman III, "The Misguided Search for the Constitutional Definition of Religion," 771 Geo. L.J. (1983), 1519.

184. Sharon L. Worthing, "Religion and Religious Institutions Under the First Amendment," 7 Pepp. L. Rev. (1980), 313.

185. Michael W. McConnell, "A Response to Professor Marshall," 58 U. Chi. L. Rev. (1991), 329.

186. Sharon L. Worthing, "Religion and Religious Institutions Under the

In the hands-on faction, Frederick M. Gedicks explicates the converse.

> [Defining religion] is important because the only way to justify doctrinally the special Constitutional protection of religion is with a theory which explains both why religion is special and why Constitutional rights are held by groups as well as individuals.[187]

> Designation of protected religious belief is, at best, an awkward one for the Court, and at worst, an impermissible intrusion into religion.[188]

SUGGESTED PARAMETERS FOR A FUTURE CLARITY

Currently, the Third Circuit, the IRS, legal commentators Jesse Choper and Joseph Dodge, and the *Harvard Law Review*, for instance, tackle the hurdle of future clarity through their own proposals. The Third Circuit prosecutes future clarity with their fourfold *Africa* criteria. The IRS maintains its Procrustean fourteen-point analysis. Choper proposes a five-point test; religion must

---

First Amendment," 7 Pepp. L. Rev. (1980), 313, 345–46.

187. Frederick Mark Gedicks, "RFRA and the Possibility of Justice," 56 Mont. L. Rev. (1995), 95.

188. See, e.g., William P. Marshall, "Solving the Free Exercise Dilemma: Free Exercise as Expression," 67 Minn. L. Rev. (1983), 545, 555–57; William P. Marshall, "We Know It When We See It: The Supreme Court and Establishment," 59 S. Cal. L. Rev. (1986), 494, 512 ; *cf.* William P. Marshall, "The Case Against the Constitutional Compelled Free Exercise Exemption," 40 Case W. Rev. (1989–90), 357, 386 (explaining the Court's endeavor to define religion is problematic because any definition applied by the courts); Weiss, "Privilege, Posture, and Protection: 'Religion' in the Law," 73 Yale L.J. (1964), 593, 604 (arguing that "any definition" would violate religious freedom because the definition would de facto dictate to religions, past and future, what they must be, hence a "chilling effect" on free expression and further running afoul of the Establishment Clause); *cf.* Mark Tuchnet, "Of Church and State and the Supreme Court: Kurland Revisited," Sup. Cr. Rev. 373, (1989), 382 (explaining that insincerity is presumed with unconventional beliefs).

first, reasonably correspond to most theological and lay definitions; second, have capacity to grow to include new or unusual sects and beliefs; third, avoid undue intrusion into persons' thoughts and behavior; fourth, aim to meet the various goals of both religion clauses; and fifth, be sufficiently specific and understandable to produce fair and uniform results.[189]

The Harvard *Law Review* drafts the following five-point screen:

(1) whether the belief system is analogous to that of conventional religions;

(2) whether it is comprehensive;

(3) the degree to which it lays claim to ultimate truth;

(4) the degree to which it is supported and identified by symbolic trappings; and

(5) the degree to which it is associated with and promoted by a visible and organized group.[190]

The value of each of these definitional schemes notwithstanding,[191] consensus building for a judicial threshold should gravitate toward three essential parameters: specificity, flexibility, and uniformity.

---

189. J. Choper, "Defining Religion in the First Amendment," 1982 U. Ill. L. Rev. (1982), 579, 580; *cf.* Note "Defining Religion," at 946–47.

190. Note "Toward a Constitutional Definition of Religion," 91 Harv. L. Rev. (1978), 1056, 1072–75.

191. Dodge offers a unique approach that dissects religion into four parts: ethical action, worship, faith, and therapy. Faith and therapy should be absolutely protected by the Free Exercise Clause, and worship should also be protected so long as there is no demonstrable harm outside the worship group or severe physical injury within it, and ethical action should receive a much lesser degree of protection. Dodge, "The Free Exercise of Religion: A Sociological Approach," 67 Mich. L. Rev. (1965), 679.

HOW CIVIL RELIGION AND GOVERNMENTAL INTEGRITY INTERPLAY

Specificity

Although the Supreme Court has been historically inclined to protect beliefs of any kind, religious or otherwise,[192] the parameter of specificity is necessary to ascertain if the First Amendment applies.

Specificity Because of the Plethora of Vague Definitions

Although the terms 'religion' and 'religious' appear in 574 sections of the U.S. Code and 1,490 sections of the Code of Federal Regulations,[193] a plethora of vague definitions in the judiciary, legislative, and commentating literature complicate determination of the specificity of claims.

> The California Supreme Court: the primary sense of religion as applied to moral questions is merely a recognition of a conscientious duty to recall and obey restraining principles of conduct.[194]

The Massachusetts Supreme Court, citing Alfred North Whitehead: religion is what the individual does with his own solitariness.[195]

Kent Greenawalt: whether something is religious is determined by comparing it to the indisputably religious.[196]

---

192. Konvitz, "The Meaning of Religion in the First Amendment: The Torcaso Case," 197 Cath. World (1963), 288, 291.

193. James M. Donovan, "Law, Anthropology, and the Definition of Religion," 6 Set. Hall Const. L.J. (1995), 23, W8 (citing a Westlaw search but appending that a Lexis search with an identical query results in 839 and 1,511 sections, respectively).

194. Estate of Hinckley, 58 Cal. (1881), 457, 512.

195. United States v. Sisson, 297 F.Supp. (D. Mass. 1969), 902, 909; Wallace v. Jaffree, 472 U.S. (1985), 38, 60–62 (holding that a moment of silence, preceded by the suggestion that one may pray, meditate, or merely think about the day, is religion).

196. Greenawalt, :Religion as a Concept in Constitutional Law," 72 Calif. L. Rev. (1984), 753.

C. Boyan: religion is description of an individual's beliefs and patterns of behavior associated with those beliefs.[197]

J. Morris Clark: religion is determined by reference to the conscientiousness of beliefs.[198]

Joseph M. Dodge: religion consists of ethical action, worship, faith, and therapy.[199]

Jesse Choper: religion is characterized by "extratemporal consequences."[200]

James Donovan: religion is any belief system that serves the psychological function alleviating death anxiety.[201]

Ellis West, therefore, concludes that the need for a clear definition is legion.[202]

Specificity as a Device for Screening Cases

Beliefs, practices, and the parties themselves must be identified as religious to determine if Constitutional protections apply. If Constitutional protections are available, to whom should they apply? By what specific standard can an individual's claim to these protections be validated? A definition of religion acts as a screening mechanism to sort out claims.[203]

With the following fourfold approach courts could determine the threshold of specificity in an orderly manner: traditional

---

197. Boyan, "Defining Religion in Operational and Institutional Terms," 116 U. Pa. L. Rev. (1968), 479.

198. Clark, "Guidelines for the Free Exercise Clause," 83 Harv. L. Rev. (1969), 327, 335.

199. Joseph M. Dodge, "The Free Exercise of Religion: A Sociological Approach," 56 Mich. L. Rev. (1969), 679, 697.

200. Jesse H. Choper, "Defining Religion in the First Amendment," 1982 U. Ill. L. Rev. (1982), 579, 591.

201. James Donovan, 6 Set. Hall Const. L.J. (1995), 23, W76.

202. Ellis West, "The Case Against a Right to Religion-Based Exemptions," 4 Notre Dame J.L. Ethics & Pub. Policy, (1990), 591 605.

203. James M. Donovan, "Law, Anthropology, and the Definition of Religion," 6 Set. Hall Const. L.J. 23, W5 (1995); Jesse H. Choper, "Defining Religion in the First Amendment," 1982 U. Ill. L. Rev. (1982), 579, 591.

HOW CIVIL RELIGION AND GOVERNMENTAL INTEGRITY INTERPLAY

theistic, non-traditional theistic, non-theistic "ultimate concern," and non-theistic functional equivalence. First, traditional theistic religions, because of their historical status, pass muster directly. Second, non-traditional theistic claims that meet the *Macintosh* standard of belief in a personal Supreme Being are sufficiently specific.[204] Third, belief systems qualifying with an "ultimate concern" in the place parallel to that filled by the traditional personal deity meet Constitutional muster. For a final "drip-pan" category, courts may determine if the beliefs, behavior, and claimants themselves demonstrate functional equivalence to the coordinates of previously accepted categories, according to a *Kauten* analysis.[205] Although the four categories move from narrow to broad, permeating any designation, however, should be both the *Ballard* sincerity and the *Seeger/Welsh* priority criteria. But, the Free Exercise Clause, of course, does not protect demonstrably secular beliefs.[206] An orderly framework for analysis would help screen claims efficiently, discouraging knee-jerk and gut reactions.

Flexibility

Professor Tribe argues that the very nature of liberty demands a definition of religion that goes beyond the closely bounded limits of theism, and accounts for the multiplying forms of recognizably legitimate religious exercise.[207] Flexibility is a necessary parameter for a definition of religion so that the rights of conscience are honored and minority religions do not suffer marginalization or a chilling effect to their expression.

204. United States v. Macintosh, 283 U.S. (1931), 605, 633–34 (Hughes, J., dissenting).

205. 133 F.2d (2d Cir. 1943), 703, 705, 707 & n.2.

206. Thomas v. Review Bd., 450 U.S. (1981), 707, 715; Giannella, "Religious Liberty, Non-Establishment, and Doctrinal Development Part I. The Religious Liberty Guarantee," 80 Harv. L. Rev. (1967), 1381, 1426 (arguing that nontheistic practices designed to advance individual psychological and spiritual development should be denied status equal to that of theistic religion).

207. L. Tribe, "American Constitutional Law" (2d ed. 1988), 14-6, 1180.

THE NEXUS OF GOVERNMENTAL INTEGRITY AND THE SURVIVABILITY

The Argument for a Flexible Scope

THE NEED FOR A FLEXIBLE SCOPE BECAUSE OF THE INVIOLABILITY OF CONSCIENCE

The First Amendment expression clauses, both speech and religion, derive from a moral philosophy that conscience is sacred. Accordingly, some legal commentators see the principal interest protected by the Free Exercise clause is freedom from governmental force to violate the compelling demands of conscience.[208] The First Amendment ennobles the priority of conscience over the demands of the state.[209] Indeed, as Justice Brennan noted the special nature of the inviolability of conscience: "rights of conscience are, in their nature, of peculiar delicacy."[210]

THE NEED FOR A FLEXIBLE SCOPE BECAUSE OF THE GROWTH AND DIVERSIFICATION OF RELIGIOUS BELIEFS

The Court has recognized that a very rigid judicial definition of religion would implicate Free Exercise concerns, especially with the plethora of new religions.[211] Accordingly, Greenawalt espouses a multifaceted analysis of religion for Constitutional purposes, arguing that no single characteristic should be regarded as essential to religiousness.[212]

THE NEED FOR A FLEXIBLE SCOPE BECAUSE OF THE DANGER OF THE CHILLING EFFECT

Justice Goldberg sees the basic purpose of the religion clauses as nurturing religious expression, to promote and assure the fullest possible

---

208. Clark, "Guidelines for the Free Exercise Clause," 83 Harv. L. Rev. (1969), 327, 340.
209. Gillette v. United States, 401 U.S. (1971), 437, 445.
210. Schempp, 374 U.S. (Brennan, J., concurring), 203, 231.
211. Note 74 Cornell L. Rev. (1989), 532.
212. Note 74 Cornell L. Rev. (1989), 532.

HOW CIVIL RELIGION AND GOVERNMENTAL INTEGRITY INTERPLAY

scope of religious liberty and tolerance for all, and to nurture the conditions which secure the best hope of attainment of that end.[213]

In the same vein, Merel argues that the single unifying principle underlying the two religion clauses is that individual choice in matters of religion should be free.[214] A broad scope, therefore, facilitates diversity by minimizing a chilling effect upon expression.

Uniformity

A uniform definition would promote consistency, an essential to fairness. Giannella agrees that a unitary definition is necessary but tempers with a plea against an unnecessary exclusivity.[215] Courts "must proceed at a level of inquiry that does not discriminate among creeds on the basis of content, [and must] not circumscribe the very choice which the Constitution renders inviolate."[216]

The Argument for a Bifurcated Definition

In Professor Tribe's original analysis, the meaning of the term religion in the First Amendment divaricates according to clause. If belief or behavior is "arguably religious," Free Exercise protection applies; if however belief or behavior is arguably non-religious, a violation of Establishment Clause may apply.[217] Under Tribe's dual

---

213. Abingdon School Dist. v. Schempp, 374 U.S. (1963), 203, 305 (Goldberg, J., concurring).

214. Merel, "The Protection of Individual Choice: A Consistent Understanding of Religion Under the First Amendment," 45 U. Chic. L. Rev. (1978), 805, 810.

215. Giannella, "Religious Liberty, Non-Establishment, and Doctrinal Development, Part I. The Religious Liberty Guarantee," 80 Harv. L. Rev. (1967), 1381, 1426.

216. Note "Toward a Constitutional Definition of Religion," 91 Harv. L. Rev. (1978), 1056, 1072-75.

217. L. Tribe, "American Constitutional Law" (2d ed. 1988), 14-6, at 1180; United States v. Allen, 760 F.2d (2d Cir. 1985), 447, 450-51 (applying Tribe's original analysis); Sheldon v. Fannin, 221 F.Supp. (D. Ariz. 1963), 766, 775 (applying different standards of what is religion depending on the popularity

classification scheme, the same facts may be labeled religious under Free Exercise analysis, but non-religious in an Establishment Clause analysis.[218] Professor Tribe, however, has recanted the earlier dual definition in the second edition of the text, explaining, "The dual definition approach . . . constitutes a dubious solution to a problem that on closer inspection, may not exist at all."[219]

Accordingly, Tribe pioneered a dualistic approach to the task of definition, arguing for a broad scope for free-exercise adjudication but a narrow scope for establishment adjudication. Echoing the earlier Tribe, in *Sheldon v. Fannin*, a federal district court in Arizona ruled that "religion in Establishment Clause adjudication is oriented toward the will of the majority and religion in Free Exercise clause adjudication is oriented toward views in minority."[220]

Despite increasing judicial support for Tribe's creative proposal, Justice Rutledge's dissent in *Everson* capsules the rebuttal of present detractors to Tribe's view.

> "Religion" appears only once in the Amendment. But the word governs two prohibitions and governs them alike. . . . "Thereof" brings down religion with its entire and exact content, no more and no less, from the first into the second guaranty so that Congress and now the states are as broadly restricted concerning the one as they are regarding the other.[221]

Hence, rebutters to the bifurcated definition appeal to the face value of the text of the Amendment. In a second prong, detractors to Tribe's view rebut that a bifurcated definition may effect special

---

of the particular religion).

218. Note "Toward a Constitutional Definition of Religion," 91 Harv. L. Rev. (1978), 1056, 1072–75; James M. Donovan, "Law, Anthropology, and the Definition of 'Religion,'" 6 Set. Hall Const. L.J. (1995), 23, W10.

219. L. Tribe, "American Constitutional Law" (1978), 828 (arguing for a bifurcated definition); *cf.* L. H. Tribe, "Constitutional Law" (2d ed. 1988), 1186 (recanting the bifurcated definition).

220. Sheldon v. Fannin, 221 F.Supp. (D. Ariz. 1963), 766, 775.

221. Everson v. Board of Educ. 330 U.S. 1 (1947), 32 (Rutledge, J., dissenting).

treatment for obscure religions, specifically allowing government greater latitude to aid such religions.²²²

The Argument for Uniform Definition

The undesirable byproduct of Tribe's analysis is the creation of three separate categories of religion.²²³ A lattice of two constitutional and one statutory definition of religion fosters judicial ambiguity. Conflict between adjudications deriving from the two religion clauses concerned Justice Brennan: "such disparity may produce situations where an injunction against an apparent establishment must be withheld in order to avoid infringement of rights of free exercise."²²⁴ Disparities of meaning breed confusion.

An Analytical Framework Rather than a Conventional Definition

Because of the abstraction and fluidity of the subject, some opine that a conventional definition of religion is impossible.²²⁵ Accordingly, George Freeman argues that some universal perception of a subject is essential to defining it.²²⁶ Anita Bowser echoes, arguing

---

222. See generally, Malnak v. Yogi, 592 F.2d (3d Cir. 1979), 197, 212–13 (Adams, J., concurring); Greenawalt, "Religion as a Concept in Constitutional Law," 72 Cal. L. Rev. (1984), 753, 814.

223. *Cf.* Malnak v. Yogi, 592 F.2d (3d Cir. 1979), 196, 212.

224. School Dist. of Abingdon Township v. Schempp, 374 U.S. (1963), 203, 230–33 (Brennan, J., concurring); Jesse H. Choper, "The Religion Clauses of the First Amendment: Reconciling the Conflict," 441 U. Pitt. L. Rev. (1980), 673 ; Kenneth L. Karst, "The Politics of Religion and the Symbols of Government," 27 Harv. C.R.-C.L. L. Rev. (1992), 503, 506 (tracing the loosening of Establishment and Free Exercise Clauses' parameters, allowing "government even greater freedom to accommodate religion" and contradiction in applying to the two clauses).

225. See, e.g., M. Elizabeth Bergeron, Note, "New Age or New Testament? Toward a More Faithful Interpretation of Religion," 65 St. John's L. Rev. (1991), 365.

226. George C. Freeman III, "The Misguided Search for the Constitutional Definition of Religion," 71 Geo. L.J. (1983), 1519, 1548.

that the process of definition is "inherently arbitrary" because a judge cannot appeal to the canons of logic to decide whether a given classification is the correct one.[227] Because classification cannot be carried on deductively, the task is an inherently arbitrary one. Andrew Austin rebuts, however, arguing that since the term is linguistic symbol in use, rules about its use are necessary.

Accordingly, a judicial framework for analysis may assuage both concerns. If the Court adopted an analytical framework, organized under the major threshold questions, "Is the claim specific enough to invoke Constitutional protection?" "Would our holding in this particular case be flexible enough to honor the inviolability of conscience and diversification of beliefs but not chill expression?" and "Would our holding in this particular case be consistent with our other holdings?" the fluidity of the subject may not be contrivedly constricted. Courts would have an appropriate elastic measure, not a Procrustean pigeonhole.

CONCLUDING REMARKS: A PLEA TO THE LEGAL COMMUNITY

Religiously motivated violence, ever-increasing in both frequency and intensity,[228] tears the national fabric. Paul Hill, the anti-abortionist extremist who murdered a doctor performing the procedures and his bodyguard in 1994, was only one portent. Because of the threat within, a coherent message from the Supreme Court that she understands that the American people are a religious people and their highest court will treat their religiosity with specificity, flexibility, and uniformity for fairness would promote social cohesion, as well as awareness that peaceful religious development

227. Anita Bowser, "Delimiting Religion in the Constitution: A Classification Problem," 11 Val. L. Rev. (1977), 163–64.

228. See, e.g. "A Convergence to Watch of Conservative Forces," *The Humanist* July 1994, at 7; Stephanie Nebehay, "Religious Extremism Is Like a Spreading 'Cancer,'" Reuters World Service, January 19, 1996 (arguing that "hate, violence, and acts of violence, including those motivated by religious extremism, could facilitate the emergence of situations which could threaten or compromise international peace and security").

HOW CIVIL RELIGION AND GOVERNMENTAL INTEGRITY INTERPLAY

is the right of every citizen. Public policy and First Amendment think tanks such as the Cato Institute,[229] Brennan Center for Justice,[230] The Rutherford Institute,[231] the Center for the Study of Values in Public Life at Harvard,[232] and the Williamsburg Charter Foundation may consider joint ventures, composed of participants fairly representing the entire political spectrum, to draft an amicus brief proposing a model analytic framework that is specific, flexible, and uniform to designate Constitutionally protected religion. Further, the same centers could consider drafting model federal legislation, including amendments to the Model Penal Code, that would propose severe penalties on religiously motivated violence. In sum, if the highest echelon of the judiciary communicates her understanding of American religiosity and uniform intention to treat religion delicately and fairly, and Congress comes down like gangbusters on religiously motivated violence, the corrective may minimize future tragedy.

In the words of President Clinton, "religious freedom is really our first freedom."[233] Pervading the Constitutional conventions were the oft-repeated, proverbial phrases, "compromise, compromise, compromise" and "thank God for the Supreme Court." The proverbial should become prophetic in the current legal arena, so that consensus building culminates in a judiciary ensuring a treatment of the "first freedom" with coherence at least equivalent to other freedoms.

Morality, that elusive quantity that everyone espouses but few dare to define, is intimately intertwined with religion. Upon ethics, the language of morality, the sea of law floats. The highest court in the land, ordained to define law, has yet to provide a workable, consistent definition of religion. A legal definition is the tip of the point of contact between law and religion. If legal coherence is essential to social order, so is a legal definition of religion.

229. 1000 Mass. Ave., NW, Washington, DC, 2001–5403.

230. NYU, Washington Square, NY, 20001–5403.

231. P.O. Box 7482, Charlottesville, VA, 22906–7482.

232. 45 Francis Ave., Cambridge, MA, 02138.

233. "Public Papers of the Presidents," Remarks at James Madison High School in Vienna, Virginia, at the Signing of the Williamsburg Charter, July 12, 1995.

CONCLUSION

The survivability of American constitutional representative democracy involves links of a chain of political ideals—integrity, credibility, legitimacy, tranquility, and efficiency. Each of these ideals is a planet orbiting the sun of morality. And religion, admittedly to varying degrees, is the fusion that powers morality.

John F. Kennedy[1] and Machiavelli[2] are correct in their assessment that morality is the strongest and most permanent force of law. Kennedy's televised statement on June 11, 1963, that "law alone cannot make men see right" rings true today.[3] Dworkin concurs: "moral principle is the foundation of law."[4] As Samson pulled the foundational pillars of the Philistine temple to accomplish its demise, so will the American constitutional republic collapse if its moral pillars crumble.[5]

1. John F. Kennedy, televised speech on June 11, 1963.

2. Niccolo` Machiavelli, "Discourses on the First Decade of Titus Livius," trans. Allan Gilbert (1965), book I, chapter 18, 241.

3. John F. Kennedy, televised speech on June 11, 1963.

4. Ronald D. Dworkin, *Law's Empire* (1986).

5. Gatgounis, G. J. (2014). *The Nexus of Governmental Integrity and the Survivability of American Constitutional Democracy*. Charleston, SC: George J. Gatgounis.

www.ingramcontent.com/pod-product-compliance
Lightning Source LLC
Chambersburg PA
CBHW071442160426
43195CB00013B/2004